STOP SELLING
&
START HELPING

The Proven Guide to Phenomenal Sales Results

BRANDON JEFFRESS

Year of the Book
135 Glen Avenue
Glen Rock, PA 17327

Softcover ISBN: 978-1-949150-53-7
Hardcover ISBN: 978-1-949150-54-4
Ebook ISBN: 978-1-949150-55-1

Library of Congress Cataloging Number: 2018963654

ACKNOWLEDGMENTS

Thank you to all of the sales reps who allowed me to invest my work into their lives. This work challenges you on so many levels and you allowed me to become a part of your success.

Thank you to the sales leaders who wanted to invest in their people and understood that if you want to grow your business you have to grow your people. Through that vision these concepts came to life.

Thank you to Tom Batchelder, who invested his work into me and introducing me to a whole new way of thinking.

Thank you to the John Maxwell Team for teaching and helping me grow as a leader. My wife Aleta for encouraging me and helping me see this through. Demi Stevens for putting her professional touch to the look and feel. Bob Hamer for correcting so many things I didn't do correctly.

CONTENTS

WHERE IT STARTED

My family was "country" poor. No suburbs, no ghettos, no urban sprawl, just barnyards and farmland. My father was the pastor of a small country church in rural Ohio, 53 miles from the BIG CITY. Our 3 bedroom wood-frame house, next door to the church, was directly across the street from an Amish school. Each day, horse-drawn buggies doubled as school buses. Boys and girls, plainly dressed, typically in black, pattern-less clothing to discourage physical appearance as a source of pride, were dropped off in front of the school. Maybe I should have taken lessons from their humility.

Being "country" poor meant that at the beginning of each school year, I got one pair of tennis shoes meant to last until the next summer. By the end of the year, I had always grown enough and worn them enough that my big toe was peeking out from the end of the well-worn shoes. The kids used to taunt me and ask why my parents wouldn't just buy me a new pair of shoes. I can still hear the jeers and jokes; their giggles and laughs echoing in my ears to this day.

I loved my dad. He preached salvation and virtue from the pulpit. He taught hard work and personal responsibility. I admired him and believed in his ministry, but I wanted the heckling to stop. Maybe that's why I admired the people in our community who created or started a business, becoming what I thought to be a "successful" person. In my mind, success meant lots of money, a title demanding respect, and the power to command the attention of others.

I guess that's why I wanted to own my own company. I wanted wealth, and I wanted to be successful. I wanted my children to always have shoes without holes. By the late 1990's, my career was exploding. I looked at the software companies I came in contact with; companies that were perceived to be growing and successful. These were the companies that people would long to work for; companies that were going public and continued growing. Each had impressive work environments and great business cultures. I would sit back and look at the presidents of these organizations, the person steering the ship, and I marveled at their success. Through my analysis, I noticed the presidents, more often than not, had one thing in common. They all had a significant background in sales. I really didn't have much experience in sales except for the brief period I sold for TruGreen Chem Lawn while in college. I had been a successful product manager for a few software companies; each of whom had been acquired. I wasn't satisfied. In my mind, I wasn't wealthy, and I wasn't successful. I wasn't steering the ship.

I believed that in order to be successful running my own company, I needed to go into sales. I can still remember going home to tell my wife, Aleta, that I needed to go into sales. I was excited with the vision, but was nervous about the jump I would need to make. How would it impact us financially? What if I was wrong? My career in the software industry as an executive was very successful. I was working for a publicly-traded company and had three teams reporting to me, but I had bigger dreams. Aleta could have easily pushed me back to the logical position, reminding me of how good my career was going with an impressive salary, stock options, and status, but she jumped on board. She knew my dream and she believed in me.

As I went looking for software sales jobs, the common response I received from potential employers was that my previous success was impressive, but they really didn't have time to train me in sales. They wanted someone with sales *experience*. While there is some truth to the concept, business executives are always selling internally to cross-functional teams in order to get the executives or board to buy into a vision, this was not the sales experience employers were seeking. Recruiters were looking for those knowledgeable in the complex sales process. I didn't have that know-how.

The president of Baker Hill was the first owner who was willing to give me a shot. Joe was the new VP of Sales. He had recently taken the position after being a sales rep for many years. I was his first hire. I took a salary that was more than half as much as I was making before. I went from six figures to about 45k per year. My dad used to say that the right sacrifices today will pay huge tomorrow. I just kept telling myself this, hoping fatherly wisdom would prevail.

Once the team at Baker Hill brought me in, they told me that because there were only six months left in the sales year, they wanted me to sit in on as many calls as I could. I was supposed to learn their business and appreciate the questions people were asking during the sales process. Over that next six months, I listened, learned, and took enough notes to make a Tom Clancy novel look like CliffsNotes. I observed totally different approaches from the various sales reps and hoped it would all make sense when I started making my own calls.

In October of that year, I took over a territory and went to work. I still remember that first day, walking into the office knowing I was actually going to be "in sales." Six months later, I sat there with one sale to my record. I was horrible and my mind was telling me to go back to product management; I wasn't a sales guy. I didn't want to tell my wife how badly it was going, but when she would occasionally ask, "When are you going to start making some commissions?" I would kindly remind her it takes time. The feeling I was letting my family down weighed heavy in the back of my mind. Maybe I wasn't supposed to be in sales. I would sit in my windowless office with the door shut, dialing bank after bank, trying to find someone who needed our product. I asked all the same questions I had heard the other reps ask, but the calls weren't turning into opportunities.

Bill Crouch, one of the other sales reps, was an energetic, outgoing guy. He always had a smile and had a laugh you couldn't miss. He was deaf in one ear and had a tendency to laugh slightly louder than everyone else. My first experience with him was watching him drip with nervous sweat during a live role-play at one of our sales kick-off meetings. I had sold one project in six months and somehow Bill was absolutely blowing out his number. He was selling projects bigger than anyone ever had before. He went from selling $35,000 projects to $350,000 projects to the same market space. How was a guy who couldn't role-play in front of his peers twelve months earlier, be blowing out his number today? I needed to know what was going on with him. One day over lunch, I decided to boldly ask the secret to his success. My exact words to him: "Bill, something is different about you. How are you doing this?"

He responded with that laugh you can't forget and said with a big grin, "You think?"

Bill shared with me that this transformation was the result of hiring a sales coach who totally changed everything he believed. Bill had hired Tom Batchelder and worked with him three times a month for the nine months leading up to our conversation. He told me about the work Tom had taken him through and how it made all the difference. Well, my mama didn't raise no dummy...I knew I needed a sales coach. I hired Tom and paid the money all on credit. We met weekly and he challenged every part of my belief system.

At the end of the year, Baker Hill had a tradition of pulling all the reps in and celebrating the year's successes. Joe, the VP of Sales, would go through each rep's accomplishments. I remember him talking about Bill. "Bill Crouch, 162% of quota."

He went through four or five big deals Bill closed that year and bragged about how Bill closed the biggest deals in the company's history for that market segment. Bill had closed the deals with revenue that would have normally taken twenty to thirty deals to reach.

The whole team whooped and hollered as the rep's accolades were shared. Then he said my name.

"Brandon Jeffress, 30% of quota."

No one clapped. No one even looked my way. The meeting was over. I learned later the reps had an over-under bet on me, focusing on how long I would make it before being fired. The lump in my throat felt like a dagger. To sit there like the kid who didn't get picked in a neighborhood basketball game and feel the failure; that feeling of being on the bottom, is a feeling I will never forget. I tried not to show any emotion as I sat there, feeling the doubt of others. I had no choice but to deal with the reality of the moment. While the others headed to the offsite party to celebrate the year, I walked into Joe's office and said, "I don't want you to say anything. I am sure you wonder if I was the right hire. I am and I will never feel like this or finish last again in my life." Without even pausing, I left his office.

Four months later I hit my annual quota, selling the largest deal in company history and the first one on our newest platform. At the end of the year, I was at 172% of quota and I never looked back. I led Baker Hill in sales over the next five years.

As new sales reps were hired each year, I watched them struggle. I could literally see them laboring with the same insecurities that caused me to feel like an outcast on "sales island." I could empathize. I saw a little of myself in their experiences. I offered to assist each rep and meet with them for thirty minutes a week to work on their craft and help any way I could. I had no desire to switch focus and become a sales coach; I went into sales to learn how to become a successful president. Even still, I felt compelled to help these reps overcome the barrier and to experience success. There was nothing for me to gain by this. None of these guys reported to me. I could simply see myself in each of them.

One by one, I worked with them and results started to happen. As weeks turned into months and months into years, word of mouth spread. People were brought into my life who were looking for different sales results and something new in their lives from a sales perspective. I took everything Tom taught me and over the years, I expanded it and created the JumpSetter sales philosophy. While I have helped countless numbers of reps, at the end of the day, it also helped me continue to grow keeping the work fresh in in my mind.

One day Aleta said to me, "Brandon, you have a gift of helping reps succeed. Why are you not charging for this?" As time went on, other leaders and experts told me I had a talent for transforming sales reps into great leaders. Many had shared with me that they believed I was on to something special with my approach. The reps I had worked with were all telling me that working with me didn't just make them successful in sales, but it had changed their lives on so many fronts. Like an epiphany, it became clear. I knew my purpose was to help people to become as successful as they wanted to become in sales. My prayer became, "God, help me to help their dreams come true."

That is the intent of this book.

I want to take everything that has been proven for so many reps, managers, and organizations, and share that as we build the foundation for enabling you to begin to reach the sales results you desire. I want to teach you to sell in such a way that will bring impact and significance to clients, teammates, and employees. As matter of fact, this book is all about helping you, no matter what role or title you hold in sales. You'll notice there are individualized sections in each chapter that will help the manager and the rep to understand each other's roles. I see so many managers who only send their reps to sales training because they feel as if they've already figured it out. One of the early lessons I learned working with organizations is that if we only work with the reps and do nothing with the managers, the reps outgrow their manager. We end up spending half the coaching time helping the reps recover from their manager's bad advice.

Learning how to change your sales methods is not going to be easy, but anything you have to build and develop that is worthwhile is going to be an uphill climb. So, if you are looking for quick fixes or a "just add water" approach to fix your sales success, you have picked up the wrong book. Please give this book away to someone who is truly interested in sustainable change and success.

People regularly ask me, "What's the one thing I need to know to be successful in sales?"

I always remind them there isn't just one thing you need to know or do to be successful. To be successful, you need to make sure your beliefs, your thoughts, your emotions, and your actions are all in sync with your team and your clients. It's important to remember that you need an intentional purpose and process to what you are doing.

Michael Drapeau, one of the top sales guys I have worked with says, "If sales were easy, there wouldn't be racks and racks of books in a dedicated sales section of all the book stores. Sales can be hard. It can also be a life-changing journey for you and for the lives you impact."

A hot topic in the market today is *Sales Culture,* and for good reason.

The best sales organizations and sales reps have established the right sales culture. Sales culture often feels like a mystical place; it isn't always tangible or easy to get your arms around.

John Maxwell, the number one expert in the world on leadership, a man who is also my friend and mentor, says, "culture eats vision for lunch at a 10:1 ratio."

Forbes magazine did an article a few years ago demonstrating that a company with the right culture will outperform its peers and competition by as much as 800%. Culture clearly matters. Culture happens when your beliefs drive your behaviors. Want to know your culture? Look at your or your team's behavior. It's that simple. Therefore, every sales organization, company, rep, has a culture. The question is: Do you have the *sales culture* you desire for you and your team? Better stated, do you see the alignment in beliefs and behaviors that you desire? Are you getting the results you desire? If so, you are probably experiencing growth at high levels and have high employee retention. My hope for you is that you can learn from my experiences to further enhance what you have.

If you don't have the results you desire, something has to change and that change starts with you. It makes no difference if you are a rep, sales manager, chief sales officer, or president. It doesn't happen by accident. It comes from design and by the intentionality of your daily efforts to have the correct beliefs and behaviors.

The president of a technology company recently told me, "Let me get my organization back on track and then I will work on our culture."

I responded, "Get your culture fixed and your organization will be back on track."

The alignment of the desired beliefs and behaviors is the foundation for the rest of this book. If you don't change your beliefs, yet try to implement these behaviors, you will fail. Again, we are not providing you magic phrases or "pick up lines" to trick your clients. However, if you buckle up and address the core of what you believe, your beliefs will drive your thoughts, and those thoughts will drive your emotions which will then naturally drive your actions. It's time to jump in!

CHAPTER 1

IT STARTS WITH YOUR DEFINITION OF SUCCESS

DEFINING SUCCESS PART ONE

Before becoming a *New York Times* best-selling author and motivational speaker, my friend, John Maxwell pastored churches in Indiana, Ohio, and California. In 1995, he left that ministry, devoting his time to leadership training and writing. He has since returned to the pulpit in Florida, but continues speaking to thousands as one of the nation's premiere authorities on leadership development. Several years ago, I was sitting on the front row facing an empty stage waiting for John to speak at one of his John Maxwell Team events. As one of his speakers, trainers, and coaches on leadership, I was sitting there like the *Karate Kid*, eager to learn from Mr. Miagi, awaiting the message he was about to deliver. Wide-eyed with an open heart, I listened intently as John spoke. During those few hours on the first day, I wrote about fifty pages of notes. As I reflect back on that day, there was one thing he shared that stood out to me.

His definition of success.

It was a definition I had not heard before. My life has been altered by his words that day. Upon hearing them, I needed to figure out what I was going to do with the information I had gained. John's definition of success is the accumulation of these three things:

- Being and staying clear about your purpose
- Maximizing your personal potential in that purpose
- Sowing seeds into others for their benefit

Before that moment, I thought of success in terms of tangible results; the bottom line on the ledger, the size of the commission check, annual bonuses. John's definition didn't sound anything like mine. He was asking me, "what was my purpose? Was I maximizing myself and sowing seeds in others?" By his definition, what I was pursuing was not success. Could I be doing it wrong? I had been told I was successful and I'd led almost every company I had worked for in sales. Suddenly, it became clear to me.

Success, in my definition, was all about my outcomes and had nothing to do with the outcomes of others. Even reading that as I write this, it sounds selfish on so many fronts. Selfish is a word that does not ever leave you with a positive connotation.

What is my *purpose*?

I was recently talking to a sales rep named Mike. Mike sells technology to the same industry in which he used to work. We were talking about the days when he was on the client side of the business. Mike recalled how he hated meeting with sales reps. Ironically, today, that's just what he is. When I asked him about his "purpose" now that he is a sales rep, he stated, "To drive revenue for my company and to convince companies in our industry to buy from my organization."

Mike's "purpose" answer is a very common response. "The company hired me to sell, drive revenue, and to sell a lot of it. Oh, and provide for my family."

You may be reading this and thinking that statement makes perfect sense. However, a few minutes later, Mike and I were talking about the sales reps that called on him when he was working in the industry. I asked him what he hated about being on the other side of that process. I kid you not, this is what he said, "I could not stand the reps who would come in and try to convince me to buy from them, knowing they had some quota to hit, and I was their ticket to success."

When I asked what he hated about that approach, he said, "Because I got no value from them. It was the biggest waste of my time."

I asked him how that experience compared to the answer he gave me about his purpose. After a long period of silence, he realized he was doing exactly what he hated. That's when I told him, "If your purpose is to drive revenue and to convince people to buy from you, then my guess is you are what you hate. How is that working for you, Mike?"

My friend realized it wasn't working. He explained that he kept losing late in the process on deals he thought he should have won. I asked him to think about the best sales experience he ever had with a rep. Next, I had him compare that experience with what he was currently doing, and I asked him to consider the gaps between the two. Things became very clear, very quickly for Mike.

The reason that clarity is so important to our purpose is because it sets the foundation for the "belief system." That belief system is the engine that drives the intent by which we show up. It is the catalyst by which our thoughts are driven. BTEA is something I am going to refer to a lot in this book. BTEA means that our **Beliefs** drive our **Thoughts**, which drive our **Emotions**, which drive our **Actions**.

If my belief in my purpose is "I am here to convince you to buy," my actions will ultimately be one of convincing the customer to buy. I've heard reps say that they want to help their customers. Sometimes they use training techniques taught by other companies and say phrases like, "I am here to help, if I can" and "I am trying to figure out if I can help you." But in reality, these catch-phrases and tactics are merely designed to convince the purchaser to sign on the bottom line. Your true intention will show itself eventually. You can't achieve sustainable success with magic phrases. The change has to start at your core... *with your purpose.*

Old Thinking: "I am here to sell."

New Thinking: "I am here to enrich you and to help you, if I can."

My purpose is to train, mentor, and equip as many sales people as I can so they can be as successful in art of sales. In my office, I have a sign that reads, "My prayer, God, please enable me to help their dreams come true."

I am intentional in everything I do towards that purpose.

Once we shift the focus off of ourselves and make it about the human on the other side, then we can be helpful and successful. In my story about Mike, he shared with me that the best experience he had with a rep was one where the rep helped him. Mike said, "He helped me become successful at what I was trying to do." Mike shared how the rep shared industry trends and best practices that his peers were working on to accomplish similar goals. The rep had put Mike's interests above his product functionality and his quota.

Each of us have the opportunity to shift our intent from one of persuasion, convincing, pushing and pulling to one of leading our clients to success even if that means our product and services can't assist them. This leads me to the second point in Maxwell's definition of success: Maximizing your personal potential within that purpose.

Defining Success Part Two

Grow your sales; Grow yourself

Now that you are thinking about your purpose, how do you maximize your personal potential in that purpose? When I had my first paying clients for sales training and coaching, I felt an obligation to be "real good." After all, they were paying for my expertise. What I was providing was no longer a helping hand, but instead, a service I was providing in exchange for fees. I had a desire to learn, to get better, and to develop tools that would ultimately enable my clients to be successful. I owed it to them to give my best. By the way, great sales people don't wing it. They prepare and realize they owe it to their audience to give it their best.

Here are five steps towards growth that you need to practice on a daily basis:

1. *Read*

   You are obviously on the right path when it comes to this step because you are reading this book. Don't stop here! You should read books, blogs, articles, and anything else that is going to help you become a better professional. Books on leadership, personal growth, and sales are all topics you can search and explore.

2. *Talk*

   Have conversations with other people in the industry. Network with clients, competitors, authors, and peers. Understanding what they are experiencing in their successes and failures will help you understand the trends that are happening in the market. These conversations should not be for any purpose other than to learn and share. This isn't about proving your worth or showing off knowledge. You are having these conversations to *learn*.

3. *Reflect*

It has often been said that experience is the best teacher. That is incorrect. A reflected view of experience is the best teacher. Review your experiences every day and let your reflection on those experiences teach you how to be better tomorrow.

4. *Create*

Write, blog, and share your knowledge with others. Every day you reach into your mind and access the information you have been learning, you are refreshing those concepts and experiences that maximize your personal potential. Every time I have trained and coached, I feel as if I have walked away learning something in the process. The process of creation enables us to actively use our mind. Plus, sharing your experiences can enrich others in the process.

5. *Be Mentored and Coached*

The best athletes in the world have a coach. I am not talking about head coaches, I am talking about coaches specific to their field. Tiger Woods has a putting coach. Lebron James has a shooting coach. Don Mattingly had a hitting coach. Olympic athletes have mentors and coaches helping them get better. Top professionals in all fields recognize the need to seek assistance from others. Have an open mind. Learn from those with varied experiences. We are all learning all the time. Those who are not constantly learning cannot help others learn.

This is why we offer coaching and mentoring as a service for our JumpSetter clients. It makes the biggest impact on our clients.

Steps one through four, should become a daily habit. At a minimum, step five should be practiced once or twice a month. Consistency maximizes potential.

When I was in college, I had a friend named Joe who started lifting weights in the university workout facility. He asked me to join him. Being that I was a whopping 5'10, 135-pound string bean, I thought I would accept his offer. I worked out with Joe the first day, doing my best to keep up; until I ran out of the gym and puked my guts out. I will never forget the experience. The football players who were walking by as they entered the gym laughed at my misery. One of the corner backs said, "Hey, keep going, that means you had a great workout."

I felt horrible and for the next three days I couldn't move. I was so sore, I couldn't walk up or down stairs or even brush my teeth. I needed a few days to recoup. Joe went day after day and I would hit it about once or twice a week. At first, everything seemed the same, but at some point Joe started to explode with growth. He was a new man, looking as if he'd been working out his entire life. I, on the other hand, had seen only minor results. Joe's consistency compounded his results, just like in your 401K where compounding interest is better than simple interest. Daily personal growth works the same way when we are consistent with it.

Sowing Seeds in Others

When I was a kid, my dad insisted on us driving everywhere we went on vacation. To some degree, it was like the *National Lampoon* vacation experience. There were many long trips from Ohio to Colorado. My dad loved the mountains, trout fishing, and visiting his mom. This was back in the days when my sister would sleep in the back window of our car, I would sleep on the floor, and my brother would sleep on the seat. We also played many road trip games. But the biggest impact on me was when my dad would play Zig Ziglar tapes. Many would be a few minutes of Zig speaking and then a positive song to support the thought, while others would be hours of Zig teaching. I remember one trip when Zig said something that caught my attention, "If you help enough people get what they want, they will help you get what you want."

I remember the day I heard that. I sat there for what seemed like hours thinking about what I could do to help people that would cause them to make me rich. I didn't fully understand the thought back then, but I wanted it and accepted it as truth. Zig nails the essence of what John Maxwell is telling us in his definition of success. If to the best of our abilities, we can sow enough seeds in other people for their benefit, we *will* be successful.

This idea rings true with most of the clients you will have in your sales career. You help them solve a problem: they pay your company for the products or services rendered, they become a reference for you with potential clients, and many times, return to purchase more. When we bring industry knowledge to a client, we are helping them. When we ask them a question that prompts them to think through their situation, we are helping them. When we share another client's story of success or failure, we are helping them. When we tell a client we're not the right company for them, we are helping them. When we have their best interests in mind and do the right thing, more often than not, we help them.

Some call it karma, the Golden Rule, or maybe even "blessed," but in my life, if I consistently do the right things for others, it eventually comes back to me. Likewise, the opposite has proven itself true.

Old Thinking: "I am going to get paid."

New Thinking: "I am going to help them even if I have to tell them I am not the right person to help them."

All of this is simple to understand but very difficult to implement. Forgive yourself if you fall back into old habits. Reflect, learn, and try again.

Reflection for the Sales Representative

1. Take time and define your purpose. If you don't know what your purpose is, meet with your best clients and ask them what you have meant to their business personally. Ask them about their best experience with a sales rep.

2. Review my five steps towards personal growth. Be intentional about what you are doing and why. If you are struggling with my five, come up with your own list of five things you are going to do every day (or consistently) to maximize your purpose and potential.

3. Think about your sales process and how you can change your focus from "qualifying and convincing" to "helping and asking questions for their benefit." You are still going to be able to qualify them. You may be surprised how they respond to your help.

Reflection for the Sales Manager

1. All of the examples I shared were for your reps. *Your* purpose is different because you are responsible for a team. Define your purpose as it relates to your team. Then define your purpose as it relates to your clients.

2. Think about my five things and what you can do for the sake of your team to become better at leading them. Come up with a Daily Five that will enable you to maximize your potential for daily growth and purpose.

3. What are some ways you can enrich the lives of your sales people? Can you invest in training, coaching, and/or tools to help them? What are ways you are enriching the lives of your clients? Be honest with yourself.

4. Sit down with your team and talk through your "purpose." Show them you are thinking about it and taking action; that you are working on your purpose just as they should be working on theirs. Don't define their purpose for them. Let them figure it out. It's not your job to figure out their purpose. If you try to impose your idea as to what their purpose should be, you will lose their trust. You don't have to be smart right now, as you might not have the correct answer for them. Let each member have his own thoughts and feelings. You will know you have their trust when they openly share with you. If they don't, it's okay, don't ask for it and don't be defensive. Reflect and learn.

5. Leaders show the way. Lead by example and share your five daily activities for maximizing yourself.

6. In your sales meetings, ask for examples of where focusing on helping the lives of a prospect made an impact on the client. Create an environment of open sharing on these things. Those who are slow to adopt will eventually learn from those who prove out the process.

CHAPTER 2

YOU CAN'T LEAD OTHERS UNTIL YOU GET OUT OF YOUR OWN WAY

Early in my sales career, I was attending a sales kickoff training session. Most companies do this at the beginning of their sales year. I am sure if you have worked in sales long enough, you have flown to a destination or to your corporate HQ so you could participate in one of these meetings. Most of the time, these events include updated product information on all the new product features that are going to help you hit your quota during the coming year. There is always a guest speaker, trainer, or motivational speaker designed to send you out to the world, inspired to accomplish new career heights in your sales year.

I am in favor of sales kickoffs and quarterly sales meetings. I have experienced some amazing training that has changed my life. Even today, I get asked to speak at more events than I can personally handle. I believe these trainings can be effective, but they can also be a waste of time. The first time I saw John Maxwell was at a sales kickoff where he introduced some concepts that framed the person I am today. Unfortunately, there have been some training sessions that make me laugh as I think back on them. Without getting into specifics about the individual trainers, as many of them are now personal friends, their whole approach was setup to fail from the moment they set foot on stage. Most of these sales experts put their focus on the words and actions that you need to change in order to become successful. As we learned in the last chapter, beliefs drive our thoughts, which drive our emotions, which drive our actions. Putting the focus on changing your words and actions without addressing the beliefs and thoughts is nothing more than a band aid approach. I am not saying you can't get any value from that approach as much as I am saying the sustainability of that type of training is questionable. My guess is that as you walked away from the training with a couple of concepts you thought you could have leveraged, you forgot about them sixty-ninety days later.

If you believe you can fake your way towards helping others with words and actions, the only person you are cheating is yourself. How often have you been in a classroom when a person asked a question, not for the purpose of getting an answer and learning, but to look smart to those in attendance? You can immediately tell their intent was one of personal engrandizement rather than intellectural curiosity. How did you respond to them? Roll your eyes? Disengage from the discussion? Speak words of annoyance under your breath? If you can pick up on such a simple display of intent, what leads you to believe that rest of the business world can't as well?

Imagine you had a long day and you finally put your two-year-old to bed. You settle down on the couch next to your spouse and the two of you are finally getting to spend some time together. Romantic feelings are just beginning when you hear your two-year-old walking out of the bedroom and laughing. What are the emotions and actions you see happening in your head? Stop reading and think about how this plays out.

What are the first feelings you are experiencing? Are you feeling frustrated? Probably. Are you feeling upset? You bet. Are you feeling happy? Not so much.

Now what actions follow those emotions? Do you march in there, pick up your child, put him back in bed and strongly encourage him to stay in bed? Some parents may even raise their voice. You have probably lost the moment you were having with your spouse. Your thought was probably the romance is being ruined, again.

The thought of the romance being ruined caused you to feel frustrated, get upset, raise your voice, and march the child back into bed.

Was this story something close to what you thought and experienced?

Now how would your emotions in this story change if it was the first time your two-year-old actually walked? A two-year-old that doctor after doctor said would never walk. What are your emotions now? Excitement? A feeling of jubilation and rejoicing? What do your actions look like? Do you run in and pick up your child and hold him close with laughter and tears flowing?

By simply changing the thought, the emotions and actions followed, even though the romance was killed in both situations.

For you to move forward, to be the best you can be, and to take full advantage of what is being shared in this book, we must help you reshape your thinking. We want the training you receive to be effective for the long term. This change in thinking is going to be about things you will work on for the rest of your life. We have all have baggage that impacts the way we think. Those thoughts don't change overnight, but over time you can begin to help yourself.

Every year, many players enter the NFL draft. They go to the NFL combine in Indianapolis where they get measured, timed for speed, and observed during agility exercises. All are fast, athletic, and usually the best players on their college football teams. What is the biggest difference between those who make it and those that don't? Hard work and mental strength are the two biggest differences; those who understand how to handle that inner voice of doubt and those who have the ability to be in a new environment with some of the same people they idolized growing up. Imagine being selected in the draft, knowing you are expected to replace an MVP or future Hall-of-Famer; playing backup to a player whose poster still hangs on your bedroom wall back home; hanging out with guys you have watched play on Sunday afternoons for the past decade. Sure you were good in college, but everyone here is good and, for the most part, have similar abilities. It all comes down to mental toughness. I've heard it said, ninety-seven percent of all people have self-limiting thoughts and fears that tell them they are not good enough. So, don't think you are any different than the President of the United States, the top draft pick in the NFL draft, the new sales manager, or the new rep hired in. Everyone is simply trying to be "good enough."

There are four common issues I have encountered while coaching some of the top sales reps and sales leaders in the country. If you can begin to understand each of these four areas and work to begin to change the way you think, you will have the mental strength to be effective. Then and only then will you be able to bring consistent value to the table; a value that will enrich the lives of people around you. You may also find that where one of these issues shows up in one aspect of life, it will show up everywhere. What I mean is, if you struggle with any of these things in your professional life, you will also be struggling with them in your personal life with your spouse, kids, or other family members.

1. Fear is always something of the future and regret is always something of the past.

When you have fear or you have regret, you cannot be in the present. When you are not in the present, you can't be fully engaged in meaningful conversation. Your listening skills go out the door as your mind allows your fear to take you some place other than where you are. If you are not listening effectively, how can you effectively help the person across from you? Do you think LeBron James was most effective with the game on the line, focusing on the shot he missed two minutes earlier or afraid of missing the next shot? When you are present, you give yourself the best chance to listen and to help.

Hint: When your emotion is one of fear, worry, or regret, you are not in the present. Pay attention when your emotions go in that direction.

Old Thinking: "I have to manipulate the conversation to control my fears."

New Thinking: "The more I just stay right here and not worry about the future or regret the past, the better I am to listen, gather information, and to help."

---

2. The biggest lie in the universe is that our value comes from others' opinions of us.

When you believe your value comes from someone else's opinion of you, more often than not, you will try to gain their approval in the wrong way. If you have seen the movie *Crazy Stupid Love*, which is a very funny movie, you will remember that one of the themes in the movie is the main character's son being in love with his baby sitter. Trying to win her over, he did things that annoyed her. His actions were causing the opposite of his desired result. As sales people, when we try to earn the respect or approval of our boss, our client, or our coworkers, we usually cause the opposite desired result. It can put you into a spiral of loneliness, emptiness, and feeling of failure when you don't receive the approval you are seeking.

However, when we stay focused on helping people, working smart and hard, and realizing our value as a human was placed in us the day we were created, it is only then we stop trying to gain the approval of others. Remember, John Maxwell's definition of success in Chapter 1 had nothing to do with personal gain and being liked.

Hint: Be aware when your desire is one of needing respect, needing to be liked, or needing to be smart. Also notice when you begin to doubt your abilities or doubt your value. If you can begin to recognize this pattern, you can then begin to renew your mind with new thinking. Self-awareness is the key.

Old Thinking: "I need my client or employees to like me, so I can be successful."

New Thinking: "My value comes from within me, which was placed there by the Creator. I don't need others to like me to be successful. If I help them, and stay true to my purpose, I will be successful."

3. **The second biggest lie you can tell yourself is that your worth is based on your performance.**

When we believe our worth comes from how we perform, we usually ride a roller coaster of emotions based on outcomes. You've probably heard the phrase "Act as if you have been there before."

When we desire recognition for our actions, we end up crushed when we don't receive that reward. If we do receive it, the prize only fuels our further dependence on it. If you let the high of a moment of success take you too high, then you will, more than likely, let the low of a loss take you too low. Someone who has been there before knows it's just a touchdown, it's just a homerun, it's just another win... it's no big deal. *Let's keep playing.*

It is those who can maintain an even keel, no matter the result, who usually have the ability to overcome with longevity. Again, the value you have comes from the fact the Creator made you exactly as you were intended to be. No amount of wins or losses changes that. The belief in this lie creates a belief that losses are bad. Michael Jordan did a commercial years ago where he talked about how all his missed shots helped him become successful. He learned from each miss. John Maxwell says "reflected experience," not experience is our best teacher. It's when we learn from our losses that we grow.

Do you remember the number two bullet in the definition of success? It is reaching maximum potential. Do we reach our best when we grow or maintain?

Hint: Notice when you have the emotion of fear associated with failure or success. Notice if you have a high need for recognition or respect based upon your performance. The ability to recognize this will allow you to reprogram your thinking. Roddy Galbraith, my speaking coach, used to say, "When you are more worried about perception of your speech than you are enriching the lives of the audience, you are being selfish and failing the audience."

Selfish performance has nothing to do with helping others. If this job isn't a good fit, you will always find another one.

Signs that you need recognition or respect to find your worth: If you feel jealous by someone else's success. If you get upset if someone doesn't mention your name. If you dominate a conversation.

Old Thinking: "I'm a failure, if I lose."

New Thinking: "I learn every time I lose and reflect on what happened."

4. **I was told a long time ago that whatever you believe is abundant, you will find it to be so, and whatever you find to be scarce, you will also find it to be so.**

One of the biggest challenges facing most people is that they think money, opportunity, and wins are scarce. Because of this belief, they attack everything in a way that creates this exact belief. When someone believes sales opportunities are scarce, they tend to cling to every opportunity. That person will act like a guy who is so afraid his wife is going to leave him that he questions her everytime she walks in the door: where was she, what was she doing, who was she with? He follows her. He checks her cell phone when she isn't looking. Over time, his actions lead her to not want to be with him and she leaves. When you believe sales opportunities are scarce, you hug them, squeeze them, and too many times, sniff the life out of them. Whereas, a guy who believes in abundance can be detached from an opportunity that allows him to stay focused on helping, even if means telling a potential client he can't help. Detachment comes when you believe there is an abundance of opportunities out there. The best sales reps are those who are detached from any opportunity and go in with a willingness to help if they can, but also have a level of skepticism and inquisitiveness. When we are attached to an opportunity, the need to sell takes over.

Money, wins, opportunities, boyfriend/girlfriend, or friends. Anything you think might be scarce, will be, if you behave as if there is a scarcity of resources.

Hint: Get up every day and be thankful for the doors that are opening. Doors that you know nothing about. Be thankful for the opportunities you currently have. Tell yourself you want to help as many people who will allow you to help. Begin to be self-aware of when you believe something is scarce in the universe.

Signs you are not detached can be noted when you use words like this: "This is a big important meeting" or "We need this one."

Old Thinking: "Money, Wins, and Opportunities are Scarce, so I need to hold on to them all."

New Thinking: "It's an abundant universe and I need to be detached from any opportunity and focus only on those where I can actually help."

Wayne Dyer, who was known for his work in transformational thinking, said, "When you change the way you look at things; the things you look at change."

This simple line is exactly what I am trying to convey to you in this process. You have to begin looking at things differently, if you want them to actually change in your life. You are not going to find more opportunities by believing there are not enough opportunities for you. You are not going to find detachment from opportunities by believing there are not enough opportunities to enable success. You are not going to have confidence and levelheadedness, if you are concerned with who doesn't like you and doesn't think you are good enough.

For the longest time, boats where made of wood because people would see sticks floating in the creek. Typically, if a person wanted a boat, he would build it out of wood. Today, we know that isn't true. Ocean liners are made of steel and you'll never see a lone piece of steel lazily rolling down a river. Once humans recognized the concept of water displacement, we manufactured metal boats that could float. And that concept didn't develop because we sat on a river bank thinking of sinking things. It came about because of created opportunities. Can you imagine if the Wright Brothers would have tried to fly by thinking about staying on the ground?

This process of renewing your mind with new thinking is a simple concept but is difficult to do. Forgive yourself if you are not successful with it the first or second time. Reflected experience is our best teacher and when we learn, we grow. For this purpose, our organization JumpSetter, has coaches and workshops designed to help you through this process. We have training and coaching geared to focus on these areas so you can work through a more detailed approach to mental strength. Until you get out of your own way, you won't be able to be truly successful.

Reflection For Sales Representative:

1. Being self aware is often difficult, but if you were to do a self evaluation what are your biggest fears in your current role?
2. Try to recognize when you have the need to fix others. What if you just focused on your personal growth and didn't see it as your responsibility to fix those around you?

Reflection for the Sales Manager:

1. What are your biggest fears about the perception of your team? How are those perceptions impacting the way you interact with them?
2. What if you were detached from the outcome of every opportunity, how would your interactions with your team members change?

CHAPTER 3

THE COMMODITIZATION TRAP

Every year, I meet with reps who complain that the market is squeezing them, consultants are pressing them, the lack of features in their product is hurting them, and on and on. It's true there are times when a shift in the market is so powerful, it hurts the industry significantly. All you have to do is look back at Apple's launch of the iPod; CDs are now a thing of the past. However, in nearly 100% of the cases where clients approached us about slumping sales, the market was not the reason they were being squeezed.

In my college economics class, a commodity was explained as a service or good that has the following characteristics:

- Usually produced and/or sold by many different companies
- You cannot tell the difference between one firm's product and another – they appear to be virtually the same product with the same value
- Typically competes based on heavy comparisons of features and functions but is heavily determined based on price

Here is a perfect example of a commodity: You are standing at your local grocery store wanting to buy a case of bottled water. As you walk down the aisle, you see five different cases, all with words like "purified" and "spring fed." All of the cases have twenty-four bottles and the price ranges from

$2.75 to $4.50 for the case. Since they all seem the same, you pick the $2.75. Gas stations struggle with this. Two gas stations side by side will often try to out price the other by one penny. In the consumer's mind, there isn't much difference in the quality of gas, so the best price wins.

Commoditization is the act by which someone's service or product is considered a commodity. Unless you are the cheapest provider on the market, you typically don't want to be viewed as a commodity. If you are being commoditized, you have no unique value or perceived value. You will be competing on price alone. It is very hard to get people to sit down with you and engage in meaningful conversation if they merely view you as a commodity. Your ability to help them is reduced significantly.

Once I got a lead from our website asking us to provide a quote for services. I emailed the customer asking to set up a time to introduce myself and our company. The email reply asked that I please just send a quote because they were too busy to talk. Clearly, in this case, my ability to help them be successful with this project was significantly hampered. I am not going to explain right now how I was able to turn this into one of my largest clients of all time, but I think it proves how being treated like a commodity hurts your ability to help.

Here are my two rules on commoditization:

- If you look, sound, and act like everyone else, you will be treated like everyone else and you will be competing on price
- The sooner you talk about your product/service the faster you get commoditized

Let's break these two down so you have a clear understanding of how most companies and reps are commoditizing themselves.

The concept of "consultative selling" has been around for years. Companies have invested heavily in training their reps to be consultative in their approach. Every rep shows up to the first meeting hoping they can quickly understand the client's situation, challenges, and goals. To speed things along, the rep asks a barrage of questions to help him understand the situation. I interview C-level people all the time who talk about the fact that rep after rep comes in doing exactly this. It is no wonder so many companies are going to RFP (request for proposal) as their choice of interaction. When you look and act the same, you will be treated as a commodity. You are nothing more than another bottle of water on the shelf.

Of course, some guy reading this is saying, "Yeah, but I am honest and really care about my clients. I am not selling snake oil."

Why is it sales people think they are the only true and honest people on the planet and their competition consists of snake oil sales vendors? News flash: most of the people out there are just like you. They are good people, trying to make an honest living, hoping for a blowout year with a ton of happy clients. Again, when you sound like everyone else, you are being commoditized.

How often do you say to a client in the first interaction that you want to understand their situation, goals, and challenges so you can best figure out if you can help? Why do you think what I write sounds like what you are saying? Because everyone is saying it. If you sound like everyone else, you are being commoditized.

What about your introduction? What do you say to introduce yourself?

"Hi, I am Brandon, I am the northeast rep and I've been here for six years. I have over twenty years of experience in the industry. Thanks for inviting us in today."

Blah blah blah. We commoditize ourselves in our introduction.

Or better yet, you tell them your company is the world's leader and you are the industry's top provider. It's redundant. Every company spews those same buzz words with zero value to the client. When everyone is saying the same thing, there is a numbness to those words. Our value is lost and we are commoditized.

My second rule is the sooner you talk or present your product, the faster you are commoditized. There are some markets where it makes absolute sense to lead with your product and offer the cheapest price. If that is your situation, skip this chapter and move on to the next chapter, as this chapter won't be of much help. However, if you are part of an organization where your product and service is a multiple- conversation process, this is an important rule you have to accept right now.

You walk into a large retailer and a sharply dressed sales guy stops you and says, "Have you seen the latest and greatest product?" Politely, you stop and listen and hear about the really cool features. He pauses, looks at you and asks, "What do you think?"

What's your next question? Exactly. How much is it?

As soon as you arrive at the price question, if you have not truly differentiated your value to the goals and challenges the client desires or is experiencing, you will be commoditized based on the price you give. Can you make a sale this way? Yes, you can. Can you consistently perform using this approach? In my experience, the answer is "no." Feel free to disagree with any of this. I am only sharing my experience from thirteen years of working with reps and organizations on these subjects. You are reading this book for a reason, most likely because your current tactics are not working. Try to have an open mind when it comes to exploring what is going to work for you.

The faster you talk about your product and the faster you demo your product, the faster the buyer wants to know the price. If you think about the way we are conditioned to buy in our personal lives then it should make sense why price is the next question. You walk onto a car lot and after walking around a desired car, you almost immediately look at the price tag. You look at the bottles of water that all have twenty-four to a pack of "purified goodness" and quickly look at the price. You go online to Amazon, search for the product you seek, and look at the price. This doesn't mean price is the only decision factor, as you may also look at ratings and opinions. But the faster you get to price, the faster you become commoditized. In business-to-business sales, rarely are the final decisions made based on all the features of your product. Usually there are four things that need to be understood by the customer in order for them to grasp the value they will get by doing business with you. If you get these out of order or skip one, you will be commoditized in the process.

- The customer has to know your personal value, and you have to be able to explain and show your personal value to the customer.
- The customer has to know the value of your company. That means you have to share your company's value

without using the buzz words and without talking about your product.

- The customer has to know your approach. They have to see their future state of success based upon your approach to helping clients.
- The customer has to know your product or service. It is your job to help them understand how your product meets their needs and goals.

I could go on and on. The rest of this book is dedicated to allowing you to not be commoditized so you and your company can be positioned well to help the lives of those you are serving in your industry. Our methods have enabled reps to go from being below average to leading their organization in sales. This methodology is proven and based on the concept that if we get out of our own way and show up with the right intent, we can then intentionally work through a process effectively with those we can help.

Old Thinking: "I have to tell them about my product and services, so I win."

New Thinking: "I can't help my clients if I focus on my product and get commoditized in the process."

Reflections for the Sales Representative:

1. How often are you being told you are too expensive? Are others in your organization selling the same product that you are being told is too expensive? If so, go and understand their process and talk about your challenges.

2. How can you change your process to not be so product/demo focused early in the conversations?

Reflections for the Sales Manager:

1. Is your team talking about your company and products too early in the process? Are you steering them to use pitch decks that are too compay and product focused too early in the process?
2. Is your product priced too high for the value it is delivering as compared to the competition? If you can't validate the value of your solution, you may be setting your team up for failure.

CHAPTER 4

KNOW YOUR PERSONAL VALUE

I was sitting in Indianapolis right where I wanted to be; in the front row of an event where Tom Batchelder, the author of *Barking Up a Dead Horse,* was speaking. He looked at me directly, called me out, and asked me a question I will never forget. He asked, "Why should your clients work with you over anyone else in your company?"

I immediately had a thought process that went like this:

I don't have the most industry knowledge, so someone with more industry knowledge might be better. Our president can make decisions on the fly without getting anyone's approval, so *he* might be better. I probably thought about four or five things other people had that I didn't have in my skill set. I responded, "I am not sure they should work with me because..." and then I shared those thoughts with him. His response was a major turning point in my career.

He told me that if I didn't know my "Personal Value" then no one else would ever know it either. I was failing my first year in sales and this guy hit me between the eyes with this response. Tom reassured me I shouldn't feel defeated because I didn't know the answer; 99% of his clients come into his training not having an answer.

I sat there with my wife next to me, tears coming down my face. How could I be twenty-eight-years old and not know my personal value? I sat there and the lecture began to fade as my mind was occupied with the question. If we don't know our value, then how is someone else supposed to confidently invest in it? It took me a couple of weeks of working through this with Tom and contemplating the subject until I finally found clarity.

If we don't know our personal value, then how can we clearly communicate it to our clients? Without us buying into ourselves, how can we expect our clients to buy into us? So, our introductions often sound just like what I shared with you in the previous chapters.

"Hi, I am Brandon Jeffress. I'm the Vice President of Sales at JumpSetter and I've been with the company for six years helping our clients with their sales training needs." Smile. Grin. Sparkle.

Am I even remotely giving my client any reason to see me differently than any other sales training sales person who walks in their door? When everything sounds the same, it is. We are commoditizing ourselves in our very first introduction. People judge you within the first seven seconds you walk into the room.

1. Do you look the part?
2. Do you carry yourself with confidence?
3. Do you connect with them?

There is a lot that can happen in seven seconds. If it were easy, everyone would be doing it. Let's dive in.

Looking the part is the easiest of the three things listed above, and I am not going to address it. Every vertical is different and knowing the proper attire is incredibly important when it comes to being received correctly by the audience you will be meeting. Research your audience, know that part, and dress it. Knowing what your role is when it comes to looking the part will help you to connect with others on a different level. We will learn more about exactly what it takes to do that in a future chapter.

If people don't feel a connection to you, they more than likely won't buy from you. Ask any woman what it is like when they have to choose a doctor who is going to deliver her baby. If she doesn't feel a connection to that doctor, then it isn't going to happen. I thought the movie *Knocked UP* really captured that concept as the pregnant mother dragged the father around to prospective doctors. She would interview them and then, based on her gut feeling, make her decision.

Let's focus on confidence. If you are not confident, it usually has to do with a few factors. There isn't anything more helpless than a person trying to sell to you who isn't confident. As a customer, you almost begin to feel sorry for him as you usher him out of the building. Here are three most common factors that will define your confidence:

1. Do you know what you personally bring as value? If you don't, then you probably shouldn't feel confident. You will never be fully confident, if you don't know your personal value.
2. Are you prepared? Did you do the necessary steps to prep for this meeting? Do you have a plan or process for handling the conversation?
3. Is your need for approval or fear of failure and the selfish need to feed your ego the focus of your intent instead of being focused on helping the customer?

Ed Decosta is one of my mentors in the sales industry. Ed speaks all over the country and has written many books. He says there are two sales a rep has to initially make in order to be successful. Those are:

1. He/She has to buy into himself. If he doesn't than no one else will.
2. The client has to buy into you as well. People don't buy from people they don't buy into.

I've worked with hundreds of individuals and have had one-on-one conversations with them. When I ask them to tell me what their "personal value" is to their client, they struggle. I don't know that I have had one person give me an answer that knocked my socks off.

I worked with a rep a few years ago who used to think he was being humble by telling the clients, "You want to talk to the smart people, I am just the dumb ol' rep."

He thought he was building up his teammates while humbling himself. You can build someone else up without dumbing down your position. You have value and they will experience it, so don't sell yourself short.

Hint: Never say the product sells itself. You might as well just say "I believe I'm worthless."

After we get most reps to begin thinking about their value, most focus on how honest and genuine they are and how much they really care about their client's success. Their introduction moves to something like this:

"Hi, I'm Brandon Jeffress, the VP of Sales at JumpSetter. I have been with the company for six years helping clients with their sales training needs. I feel like I bring my clients an honest approach because I really care about my client's success in these projects."

Now that is definitely better than the first introduction, but I think we are still commoditizing ourselves. The majority of the world is just like you and me. They are people who get up every day, go to work, want to be successful, and care about their client's success. Sure, there are swindlers and sleazy sales people out there, but the majority of people are just looking to balance personal successes with their client's successes. However, 99 out of 100 reps have told me their biggest value to their clients is their honesty and that they truly care about their clients. If everyone thinks the same and sounds the same, you will be commoditized.

So, how do you find what your value is to your clients? I usually recommend my clients start off by asking themselves the following three questions:

1. What did you define as your purpose in Chapter 1? How you view your purpose in your role as it relates to benefiting your clients should go a long way in helping you understand the value you bring.
2. Based on my own personal buying experiences, what are my beliefs as to what a good sales person should bring to the table?

Hint: Think back to your last few purchases either professionally or personally and describe what a good experience was and was not.

3. What are the core things you feel your clients experience by working with you? What would your clients say about working with you?

Hint: Go ask them! If you don't, you are skimping on the process. Skimping on the process is not maximizing yourself.

You should have an idea of what your purpose is, what your beliefs are, and what your clients say about you.

Now, here is something I am going to share with you that we have found to be true. I am going to share this more than once in this book and the reason is because it is extremely subtle but extremely important when it comes to being an effective communicator. The more you share your words and stories from your client's point of view, the more believable you are. When you say, "Here is what I think you should do," you are selling. When you say, "Here is what my clients found to be helpful as a next step," you are consulting.

Which do you want to be? A sales guy or someone who helps? So take your purpose, beliefs, and what your clients say about you and write a two-minute introduction. Introduce yourself and share your purpose/beliefs and how your clients say that has helped them. It should sound like a story and not like a script.

By realizing you have value, you won't have to "pedestal" the client to a point where you feel like you must thank her for her time. No need to lower yourself simply because the client has money and you want it. You'll know you're pedestalling when you cower and cater to every whim. We have to be on equal playing fields to be able to help. When you recognize your own value and truly believe in it, then and only then, are you able to focus on the client and in turn, the client should see you as a person who can help and enrich the lives of others. A person who is not confident will rarely be seen as a person who can enrich lives. It's through this belief in your purpose and value that your confidence can flourish.

I know you were probably looking for it, but I am not going to share with you my introduction. My introduction is not your introduction. Mimicking mine will not bring belief to how it actually fits for you. I urge you to resist the shortcut. There are no shortcuts in life. Paul Martinelli, the president of the John Maxwell Team says it best, "The long way is the easy way and the short cut is the hard way."

Again, it's got to be all about you and your belief in your personal value and what previous client's have said about you, your company, and your services. There are no magic phrases in this approach.

Old Thinking: "I am just the sales rep."

New Thinking: "I know my purpose and value and I am an expert in conveying it."

Reflections for the Sales Representative:

1. Be honest with yourself, do you really know what your personal value is?
2. Do your teammates know what their personal value is when they introduce themselves in your meetings with your prospects and clients? Take time to explain this chapter to them and help them introduce themselves effectively.

Reflections for the Sales Manager:

1. Your personal value is not your title even though it may open doors for you. What is your personal value that you bring to your clients and to your team?
2. What if your value has nothing to do with you being the smartest sales person in the room? How would that change the way you answer questions or assist your team?

CHAPTER 5

KNOW YOUR COMPANY'S VALUE

I was in a meeting with a good friend named Paul. He was VP of Sales for an application development company who writes applications and hosts them on the web for their clients. We were talking about his situation and I asked him to share what he felt was the value of his company.

He said, "We help our clients communicate better and more effectively with their employees and audience by leveraging today's latest technologies."

Those words rolled off his tongue like he had shared it thousands of times before. I asked him how that message was any different than that of Nextel Communications and their new walkie-talkie phone system. If you remember, Nextel had these phones that also worked as a walkie-talkie and allowed you to talk instantly to the other person without placing a call. I remember Paul's face turning ghostly white.

"It doesn't sound much different at all."

I shared with him that if you don't sound any different, then you aren't different and that's when commoditization takes effect. Paul invested in sales training and coaching the next week.

Most organizations want to focus on two areas as their core differentiators when explaining their value:

1. Product
2. Quality of their service

The challenge with both of those items is that someone may have the pink button where you have the blue button and "quality of service" is something everyone touts. Even the organizations with horrible reputations for service claim to be world-class services. I find those two things are very hard to differentiate by themselves. You already learned that the faster you talk about your products and services, the faster you get commoditized. You also know that when you get commoditized, you hinder your chances of being helpful to the client.

In my experience, the biggest value your company has are: the stories you can share, what your clients would say about you, and what you have learned through successes and failures. It's not your marketing documents, product demos, or your name in the market. All of those things can ultimately be commoditized. What can't be commoditized is what your clients are saying about you. Commoditization can't happen through the stories of your successes and how your organization has become better through failures. We are not sharing the stories to convince the client to do business with us. If that is our intent as means of persuasion, it will come across in the way we share the story. Let the story be there to help the client learn through someone else's experience. Just because it was a great story for one person does not mean a new prospect will identify or agree with it. That is the beauty of detachment. You have the ability to share what you have learned through both successes and failures. While those points are key, failures may be your biggest value of all.

My wife and I have a wonderful daughter named Alyssa. She graduated from the University of Northern Iowa where she was a college softball pitcher. Since she was nine, she has worked on hitting and pitching literally every week of her life including Christmas week and vacations. She fell in love with being a softball pitcher. After leading her freshman high school team to a state championship in softball, expectations went sky high for her. One day her elbow started hurting and her arm began swelling and turning blue. We went to several doctors to have it examined, concerned for her personal well-being and her future career in the sport. Alyssa loved softball so much, she majored in coaching and exercise science with a goal at that time to one day be a Division I softball coach. Our concern for her ability to keep pitching was there as well. We met with many well-qualified and reputable orthopedic surgeons. The doctor who stood out was the one who talked about this rare condition he had seen before and how he only recognized it after initially diagnosing it incorrectly. Through the process of having to go through two surgeries before figuring it out, he learned how to differentiate the difference between the more common situation that causes this and the very rare condition. He then said, "My guess is that you don't want to go through two surgeries to get a successful result unless you need to?"

Some of the other doctors thought her injury was more common. He was the only surgeon who was able to explain how his previous failures enabled him to now successfully diagnose the condition every time. You guessed it! We picked that doctor. She did, indeed, have the rare condition requiring surgery where they had to remove a piece of her rib that was pinching a nerve against the pectoral muscle. His ability to share the story helped us tremendously and it made us trust him. This is a great example of someone enriching us through the act of helping us make the best decision. Failure stories are part of your company's value and when you share them correctly, you help educate and enrich the person whose job is on the line for this decision.

The answers are not in the building.

I went to Pragmatic Marketing Training back in the 1990's when I was the Director of Product Management for a software company. The first day of the class, the instructor stood in front of us with a slide that read, "The answers are not in the building." This meant that as smart as we might think we are at knowing our clients and the market, we are not smart enough. We need to get out of the building and hear from the clients, whose opinions count the most.

The same thing matters when it comes to understanding your company's value. Don't turn to your marketing materials as they are built in house. Go sit down with your best clients and ask:

- What was it that stood out about the way we do business that caused you to see yourself being successful in this project with us?
- What was it that we did differently than the other companies you met with?
- Besides our product, what was it that our references told you about us that resonated with you and affirmed your decision to do business with us?
- What was it you were most looking for in a provider that you found to be true with us and validated your needs being met by doing business with us?
- What did you learn from us that no one else taught you in the entire process?
- What was it about the process that we put you through that you found to be most helpful and gave you confidence that we were the right company to work with?

Most sales reps and sales organizations don't know these answers because they don't ask. So don't beat yourself up too badly, if you fall into that category. By the end of this book, you should know how to have this type of clarity before the contract is signed. Also, don't be surprised if the client does not always know the answers to these questions. The answers are there though. Help walk them back through the experience and take them through the journey again. You want to be very careful not to lead them to the answer *you* want to hear. People will take the easy way out and if you lead them to an answer, they will, more often than not, take it. You rob them of their clarity and revelation as well as your ability to get the truth. Be patient. If they don't have an answer, ask them to think about it and get back to them.

Watch out for the client who wants to make it about your product. They love to talk about the tools, but it's not the reason they truly selected you. It's okay to have some feedback about your product, but that's not the purpose of this exercise. "Product value" is different than "company value." Also watch out for them wanting to add buzz words or generic answers in response.

An example of that would be, "Your reputation in the market was so good we just felt comfortable with your organization."

While that tells you that reputation is important it doesn't really have much meat to it. So following up with additional questions like, "Why was our good reputation so important to you personally as compared to a company who is less known?"

The goal, just like in personal value, is that you will be able to share in your client's words exactly what value your client experienced. An example would be that Bob told you this was an important decision for him in his career. He picked you because your reputation was so important and he could not afford the personal risk of not going with a proven organization. I then could say to someone, "I often hear from our clients' decision-makers that their personal reputation was on the line in making such a big decision in the market place."

Therefore, our clients talk about the fact that our reputation in the market helped them feel a little more at peace with a proven, successful organization. Knowing your company's value from a client's point of view helps the prospective buyer relax. She may also learn what she should be considering in her decision and had not. It can validate what the client is looking for in a provider. It can also point out that what they are looking for is not what your clients find as a value for you, identifying a possible reason to not do business with you. You want to help a client see how they sound different from your other clients. In later chapters, we will cover how to use this value data to guide C-level conversations, leveraging these insights.

Go talk to the gray beards.

In many movies, the guy with the longest and grayest beard is usually the wisest man in the village. In your organization, the reps who are consistently having the most success for the longest period of time will probably have knowledge of the company's success and failure stories. This is a next best option if, for whatever reason, you don't have access to the clients directly. I still recommend both, as this is how you learn. Don't be surprised if their answers are not as concise as you would like and if the answers tend to be a little vague. The best thing you can learn from them are the stories.

Start off by asking about the biggest failures he has suffered in client implementations and client experiences. Find out what he learned and what the company changed to overcome that situation in the future. I was working with one of my clients who sells "disaster recovery" as a service. They specialize in hosting complex DR for virtual and physical environments. While working with one of their newer reps and putting him through this process, he learned that last year their company had a major implementation issue with layer two and layer three networks causing a massive delay in their implementation for a client. By working through that issue, they learned how important it is to have a much deeper level of conversation around a network design based upon the scenarios they were trying to protect against with their DR plan. Through the process of explaining to new perspective buyers the need to discuss this topic at a deeper level to avoid the previous experience, they learned that their competition was not having this conversation. This is now one of the biggest values they bring to their client and it truly differentiates them in the market. This all came about because, the newer sales rep asked their most seasoned reps about one of his biggest client failures and how the company learned to overcome it. Hint: Also, ask the veterans about the stories they share the most and why they like those specific stories.

Mark Hill, the original founder of Baker Hill, once shared with us that as reps we needed to have three stories ready on demand that would be relevant to the prospect we were calling on. It was so vital to our success, he said, "If I am on a client call with you and you don't share stories, you may have to find your own ride home."

The point I am trying to make is that these stories are the true value of your organization. You have to know them to convey your company's value. People pay when the value they expect to get is more than the investment. Commoditization happens when the value is perceived to be the same across all providers and therefore the cheapest wins.

> *Old Thinking: "My product features and great quality service is my company's value."*
>
> *New Thinking: "The best way for me to share my company's value is to share about my clients and stories of our successes and failures."*

Reflection for the Sales Representative:

1. How many stories do you even know about the impact your company has made on it's clients?
2. How many stories do you share? Do client's ever respond and share feedback to any of your stories? If not, they may not be resonating with them.
3. Who is the best story teller in your company? This is the person that when they are talking, most people are laughing and responding with laughter and positive energy.

Reflection for the Sales Manager:

1. How can you facilitate the sharing of stories across your team?
2. Are you a good story teller?
3. How can you improve you and your team's ability of telling stories?
4. Who is the best story teller on your team? How can you leverage them to help the rest of the team?

CHAPTER 6

THE IDEAL CLIENT

I shared the story of Bill Crouch in the introduction of this book. When we were selling software projects with a total contract value of $30,000, Bill sold a project in California for $350,000. This was a great milestone because in the segment of the market he was serving, that had never been done. Bill and I set up a time in my office to discuss this project. He began to share how sophisticated this client was in their thinking, approach, and incentive programs for their employees. He went on to tell me how they planned to use our software solution to move their organization forward. Bill, in a very clear fashion, shared not only the client's culture and strategy, but also how we fit into it. I was quickly writing down everything he was telling me and drawing on the whiteboard. This was before cell phones had the camera capabilities of today, so I couldn't record our conversation or take a picture.

Over the next few days, I studied what Bill had shared with me. I set up another meeting with Bill where I attempted to tell the same story on the whiteboard to make sure I had captured exactly what he was communicating. After acknowledging I had nailed it, we both realized this was our ideal client.

Some people mistake their target market with their ideal client. Your target market is typically the demographic information that surrounds the clients you are targeting. Your ideal client has more to do with the strategy and culture of the clients you are targeting. Each of these plays a role in targeting the clients you want to attract as new customers. The illustration below shows clearly how each factor encompasses the client. In addition, it defines how culture and then strategy get to the heart of the ideal client and where there is alignment or fit.

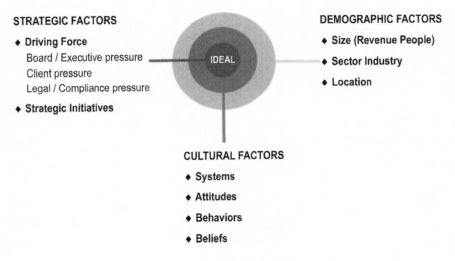

STRATEGIC FACTORS

♦ **Driving Force**
  Board / Executive pressure
  Client pressure
  Legal / Compliance pressure

♦ **Strategic Initiatives**

DEMOGRAPHIC FACTORS

♦ **Size (Revenue People)**

♦ **Sector Industry**

♦ **Location**

CULTURAL FACTORS

♦ **Systems**

♦ **Attitudes**

♦ **Behaviors**

♦ **Beliefs**

Figure 1: Ideal Client Factors

Bill figured out a way to clearly and succinctly communicate what he envisioned our new ideal client would look like. For Bill to hit his quota under the $30,000 project size, he would have had to sell twenty-five of those projects. With the proof that this new project was possible, he only had to sell five $30,000 projects and two of the larger projects. If he could sell more than that, he was blowing out his number. He did. Bill met 162% of quota that year.

We sat there in his office after I drew out the client story. We realized we needed to evangelize this story to the market. In today's market, there are a number of different philosophies about selling: Solution Selling, SPIN Selling, Consultative Selling, and Challenger Selling.

"Challenger Selling" was closest to what Bill and I discovered. We needed to communicate to other companies about what our top clients, their peers, were doing to be successful (without being specific to the actual client name). If we went out and taught other executives what our best clients were doing, then we were educating them on market trends and challenging their thought processes and buying styles.

The first company I decided to try this on was a $170 million bank in Texas. The president of the bank had instructed a young lady to reach out to us about one of the modules of our software solution. After a brief conversation with her, it was clear to both of us, she was in over her head. She couldn't answer my questions and she didn't connect with anything I was sharing. After our call, I immediately called back the bank and asked for Jim, the president. Expecting to leave a voicemail, I was shocked when he picked up the phone. About five minutes into the conversation, I shared my method of what typically helps my clients. That method included the process of taking the time to sit down with the client and share the market trends we were seeing our best clients implementing. This helps my clients to understand the culture that their business is a part of and to learn the strategies other businesses are utilizing. The prospective client can see how well their company aligns with the others. If you do align, we can probably help, if you don't, we may be limited in our ability to help. Jim agreed to a ninety-minute meeting with me.

Two weeks later, I flew into Texas and drove to meet Jim at the bank. I walked into the board room and realized this meeting was only going to be between Jim and me. In the past, when I sat down with other presidents or top executives, the conversations often felt awkward. I would ask questions and they would answer. Throughout the process, I felt like I was probing for cracks to wedge myself into, and they clearly didn't want me doing that. Many times reps show up and ask consultative questions and the person on the other side of the table doesn't get any value out of the conversation. We will talk about this in our chapter on how to differentiate early. This conversation with Jim was different. I shared with Jim that I wasn't sure if I or our company were the right catalysts to help him with his end strategy, but I could help him understand what our best clients were doing and maybe help him adjust his strategy.

There are two types of help we bring as sales reps. The first type is that we can enrich them by helping to shape their strategy, thinking, buying methodology, understanding of the competitive landscape, and trends in their industry. The second is, if there is a fit, we can sell them something that will help enable that strategy.

Hint: Jump to the second one and you commoditize yourself.

I was focusing on the first type of help. I went to the board and began to share the story that Bill Crouch had shared with me. I drew it out and articulated the culture and strategies of the clients we help the most and did it exactly how I had rehearsed it. Jim asked a few questions during the process and I then began to ask questions. I did it, not from a point of qualifying, but of helping him think through his current situation, comparing it to what it could be. Jim was contemplating, writing notes, and listening. Finally, he opened up and began to brainstorm with me. I shared a few specific client success stories from Texas and talked about Steve Vaughn of Texas National Bank in Tomball, Texas.

Steve was a very progressive president who was one of my best clients. At the end, Jim asked me the one question that changed the game. He asked me, "How can you help me be more like that bank?"

Honestly, I had not thought that far. Off the cuff, the best way I knew to help the client was to get them to our corporate headquarters and put them around the smartest people we had. Jim agreed to that as a next step. Two weeks later, I picked him and his executive team up at the airport in Indianapolis and drove them to our corporate headquarters. Jim shared how he spent one day last week meeting with Steve Vaughn and was blown away by what he learned. He was 90% sure his bank was moving forward with us. I had no idea he would take the initiative and visit Steve on his own, but he did. Jim went on to buy more than $200,000 in solutions from me and my company. One year ago, I would have worked with the lady he sent to inquire and would have eventually sold them a $30,000 project.

Not every meeting went this way. I remember meeting with a potential client in Fort Worth, Texas who laughed at the ideas I shared. I also had a meeting with a client in Austin, who sounded like Jim, but was all talk. I quickly learned I had to be skeptical. Many people would be "all talk" who would talk-the-talk but wouldn't be willing to make the changes. It's like all the people on New Year's Day claiming they want to lose weight but four weeks later are eating fried food and have stopped working out.

I learned I had to figure out how to help people in all phases of their business because not everyone was willing to take on the larger project even though they talked a big game. I sold a number of them $60,000 and $90,000 packages because that was what was right for them based on where they were in the process. Some people make the mistake of believing that if someone doesn't align perfectly to the ideal client, you ditch them and move on. I believe we have to meet people where they are and help them move as much as they are willing to move. Some people, just won't allow you to help them and that is okay, too. We can't help everyone. We can only help those who are willing to change, grow, and potentially consider things differently than before. We have to stop chasing rabbits we can't catch. The faster we identify an organization we can't help, the less likely we will lose late in the process and waste time. That is, unless they are in perfect alignment with you from the beginning which happens too.

Just two months later that's exactly what happened to me. I sold the largest project in the company's history to a client in this market segment. It was a $575,000 project. These two projects put me over quota and that was great, but not as great as knowing I was helping the lives of people whose livelihoods were at stake.

The universal law of attraction basically says that the more clearly you contemplate and define what you are trying to attract, the more likely you will be connected to it. Joel Osteen says that the more specific and thankful you are about what you desire in your life before its provided to you, the more likely God will reward your faithfulness in his ability to provide. Many other religions and philosophers have written and taught a similar belief system. My experience is that the more clearly you understand your ideal client's cultures, strategies, and beliefs, the more you can educate the rest of the market to what success trends looks like.

In the technical, software, and complex sale world where many of us live, too many reps and organizations put the focus on technical or functional fit. Our experience is that 50% of the buyer's process should be focused on whether this is a strategic and cultural fit and 50% of the process should focus on technical fit. If there is not strategy and cultural alignment, it is ill-advised to move forward, even if there is a technical fit. Our reasoning is that typically you will get commoditized and have to compete on price, or if you do get them as a new client, they will probably make your life miserable.

To understand your ideal client, you have to focus on the three areas provided in Figure 1 earlier in this chapter:

Strategic Factors

I always recommend talking to the reps who have sold the biggest and most complete projects. These projects are typically well-profiled within your organization. I encourage you or your organization to meet with this client and learn the following in detail:

- What was the driving force behind the project? What business situations, inside and outside of their organization, were impacting them to do business with your organization?
- What did they believe they could accomplish or what was the strategy-outcome of making the change?
- What compelling events caused them to take action now? What was the epiphany that caused them to say, we have to do this now and can't wait six, twelve, or twenty-four months?

Cultural Factors

"Cultural fit" is a factor many sales reps skip over. When I talk to the clients I had the most success with over the years, the common theme is they felt there was alignment between their beliefs and mine. Culture is where beliefs align and desired behavior is the outcome.

Culture = Behavior

As we did in the strategy section above, we are talking to our best clients.

- Understand what they expected in the buying process versus what they actually experienced with your organization. What was the value they received? What changed their perspective?
- What were their biggest fears, personally and as an organization, going into this project?
- How were they prepared to address change management or the impact on their people with this change? If they were not prepared, what was it they were looking for in a provider to specifically help in the process?
- What was the biggest difference in the attitudes of the people who were seeing this project through versus those who were just along for the ride or not strongly in support of the project? What was the biggest catalyst for the attitudes of those supporting the project? How did history of other projects impact those attitudes and how did they try to align beliefs ahead of time to get buy-in across the board?

There are other factors, but these will help get you started in this process. Again, you want to understand what they thought about "strategy and intentions" behind their "attitudes and behaviors," not what they liked about you, your company, or your product.

The purpose of ideal client selling is not to have the rep talk 80% of the time. The purpose is to educate the client, build rapport and credibility, so the client can learn and effectively talk for 80% of the time about his company. This is not about you showing up, telling a story, and everyone whipping out their credit cards and signing contracts. The sharing of these insightful trends of how best-clients think and behave will impact those you can ultimately help the most. This is the art of telling a story and connecting with your audience in a way that helps both of you. It is about educating the client, showing them how life could look, and understanding the gap between where they are and where they could be. The key to this is making sure you are not chasing a rabbit you can never catch. We will talk more about this in Chapter 9.

Old Thinking: *"I can sell to anyone who has the problems I solve."*

New Thinking: *"I am better served to help those who align strategically and culturally and have the problems we solve."*

Reflection for the Sales Representative:

1. With the popularity of the "Challenger Sales" model, most reps think they are there to challenge the client to believe differently. I don't believe we can turn Republicans into Democrats or vice versa. Our role is to evangelize, educate, and help those who are open and willing to do what is necessary to be successful with change. Be aware of your desire to change someone instead of meeting them where they are.

2. Do you really understand who your ideal client is and what he looks like? Do you understand the trends in strategy, beliefs, and behaviors and culture those

clients possess that truly enable them to be so progressive and forward-thinking? Do you understand what the beliefs and strategies are of a client who won't do business with you or where they did but failed with your organization?

3. Practice with your co-workers by presenting this in a whiteboard fashion instead of a PowerPoint presentation. There is something about a whiteboard conversation that makes people feel as if it has been more consultative than a PowerPoint-canned presentation. Get feedback and be prepared to teach others after you experience success.

4. Reflect on the deals you have lost late in the process. It's not always the case, but there is usually a sign that there was not enough "fit" for you to work on that particular project. Reflect and use what you learn to help you in the process moving forward.

Reflection for the Sales Manager:

1. I often hear that sales managers force their sales reps to chase too many projects where the client's culture for buying, thinking, and strategies do not align with other successful projects. Their reasoning is often that you stay in long enough to figure out how to win. The pressure you receive from your boss to sell more is not a reason to chase rabbits you cannot catch. This thinking will destroy trust between a sales rep and a sales manager.

2. Seek to understand why your reps feel the need to remove themselves from a project or why they need to stay in a project. Let the reps learn to fish.

3. Don't be so quick to tell them you were right and don't be so proud to refuse to admit you were wrong. It's not about you, it's about the reps learning how to think,

understand, and behave. Telling them what to do robs them of the ability to learn.

4. There is a wise saying: "There are many who will tell you what to do, but few who will help you grow up." Telling them what to do does not make them better. Ask questions that help them to think, even if what they decide is different from what you believe. Avoid asking leading questions. Leading the witness is bad coaching and destroys trust.

5. Get as involved as your reps in understanding who your ideal clients are. Help them to figure it out. Foster open discussion. Don't test them. Offer to do the same presentation to get better yourself. Notice if your fear of performance causes you to not want to participate but to facilitate only. You are a team and you all need to be in this together.

6. Remember the answers to success are not in the building. Talk to your clients. Meet with them. Learn from them. I can hear the VP of sales saying, "We are in too big of a hurry to meet and talk. It will take too long. We need to move forward now and not waste time reviewing past successes and failures." I love this John Maxwell quote, "The short cut is the hard way and the long way is the easy way." Short cuts are for people who are willing to put the end result at risk in order to receive immediate gratification. Help the team get it right and watch your results change.

CHAPTER 7

CONNECT

From the 1950's through the 1980's, "relationship sales" was the talk of the sales industry. That concept simply meant that if a rep would just develop a friendship, the client would buy from you. During that time, business people would buy from their friends only to realize that buying from friends didn't always turn out the way they had hoped. Organizations began to pass internal rules stating you could not buy from those in whom you had a vested interest, because the employee's ability to make a solid decision was blinded by their commitment to the friendship. It's likely you have heard sales leaders push their teams away from relationship sales.

People do not buy from friends; they buy from those they trust to deliver the solution for the right value. This chapter is not about trying to become your client's best friend. Instead, this chapter is about the importance of connecting. Just because you connect with someone does not mean they will do business with you. When you connect with someone you earn the opportunity to have meaningful and truthful conversations, giving you opportunities to help and enrich others that you wouldn't have normally have access to. I call these "at bats." You can't just stand there and wait for the opportunity to run. You have to hit the ball and if you were not in the batter's box, you wouldn't be in the game. Connecting gives you the chance to help.

John Maxwell wrote a book called *Everyone Communicates, Few Connect.* When I read the title, the message was clear. I was twenty-years-old and still in college, when I decided to join one of the nation's largest multi-level marketing companies. I went after that job with passion and dumb faith, believing I could do it. I also had a willingness to do what other successful people in the company told me to do. I listened and I learned. Within two years, I had many people from all walks of life in my business organization. I remember when I was with one of my up-line leaders on a house call to visit the CEO of a major company in Indiana. Looking to diversify his income, the CEO was open to learning about the business. I walked into the meeting proud that at my age I was getting these types of meetings and hoped my super successful up-line leader would be impressed.

At the end of the meeting, a blanket of exhaustion hung over the room. I was spent. After shaking hands and saying our goodbyes, I walked out of the house with my up-line sponsor. He looked at me and said, "Brandon, you talk way too much." I did a bunch of communicating, but I failed to connect. Too many reps talk way too much. Connecting isn't about talking, it is about having the ability to let the other person feel and identify with the value of you. When that person on the other side of the conversation feels you value them and you bring value to them, you connect. It is when we connect with people that real communication begins.

I was working for a financial services firm based in Boston. I flew into town for my initial start date so I could attend HR meetings and training. It was my first day on the job and I was notified an RFP (Request for Proposal) came in from a client in my new territory. I set up an initial conversation with the contact, so I could introduce myself and learn about the project. The lady on the other end of the phone was named Sandy and she was very formal in the way she communicated. She spoke in a voice that was very "procurement-like," even though her title was "Senior Project Manager." Sandy filled me in on all of the basic information, hoping to entice us to complete the RFP. Not knowing much, as it was my first day, I went through my "personal value introduction" and proceeded to tell her this was my first day on the job.

Sandy informed me she had only been hired forty-five days prior to taking on this project. I asked her about where she came from and what she was most excited about as it related to her new position. She informed me it was a huge opportunity to help this organization and it was a very high profile project. I don't know what was different in my mind that day (maybe, because it was my first day on the job), but I felt empathy toward her. We discussed the next steps on the project and we ended the call. Later that day, I drove to the local drugstore on my way to my hotel and purchased a *Congratulations* card.

I congratulated her on the new position and then wrote, "Sandy, I only have one goal in this project. No matter if we are the right company to help you with the end solution or not, I want to help you be successful on this project."

Before that day, I had never handwritten a card like that. I sent it out. I've often wondered why I did it, because it wasn't a tactic. I simply wanted to be nice. I was able to empathize with her in a new position, as I was feeling the pressure of me fulfilling a new position. I didn't think much about it, but a week later I got a call on my cell phone from Sandy. She was in tears and told me how much that card meant to her. She was touched that I cared about helping her that much. She told me how she wanted to help me out as well. Sandy became my internal coach and helped me win that project.

When it closed six months later, it was the largest project in the company's history. I *connected* with Sandy.

I have shared this story many times and I have often had reps tell me how they have tried to send a similar message after their first calls with clients and it didn't work. Connecting is not a magic formula you do by writing cards and saying mystical phrases to put people in a trance to feel your value. The connecting must be real.

There are three things that have to exist to connect with someone:

1. Focus

Great connectors understand that connecting can only happen when you shift away from your personal desires and keep your complete focus on the client. It is all about them. This is why people who try to take the words I shared above and use them, don't have success. Their intent is transparent, viewed as a trick to convince the potential client to open up the corporate wallet. It's like a cheesy pick up line. Interestingly enough, I have not sent another handwritten card like that since. I guess it didn't feel like the right thing to do.

In the story about Sandy, I realized her fear of failure and her need to prove herself in a high profile project was the one area I could help her. That had nothing to do with my company, my product, or our eighteen years of proven history of "yada, yada, yada." My success had to do with helping her be successful in all facets of the project. Her insecurity on this project showed me she could potentially need my help. After all, I had a long history of helping business people who were in similar situations.

To be focused on someone else, we must first push our personal desires to the side and that takes a secure person. If you are insecure, don't bother trying. You will only further hurt yourself in the opportunity. Insecure people can only think about their needs and desires. They let their fear of losing or failure dictate the conversation. They let their need for respect or recognition drive their intentions.

Think back to the purpose you defined for yourself. On what part of being selfish did you focus? Selfishness and being focused on someone else don't go together. When we are insecure, we put selfish needs above our ability to help others.

"Where selfishness starts, leadership stops."

2. Effort

Connecting with people doesn't come easy, it takes effort. It takes energy. If you want to connect with people, it isn't going to happen by simply walking into a room and saying a few lines. Unless you already have a known personal brand and history, you won't connect that easily. It is not in my nature to buy a greeting card. The last thing I wanted to do was stop by a drug store on the way to my hotel room. I wanted to have dinner and enjoy some evening sports before calling it a night. While it was not a lot of work, it was *effort*. You know, it's not hard beating the average sales rep. The average sales rep does the minimum. The average sales rep focuses on his needs while pretending to care about the client's needs. To beat the average person, you have to give effort, maybe not a lot, maybe not even the "extra mile," but it takes some effort to extend a hand. It's not just a sales ploy, it's called "being human."

There were four other nationally-known companies actively involved in that opportunity with Sandy and her company. Sandy shared that I was the only one who offered to help her personally to be successful in this project. I worked with a rep a few years ago who had been a 100% producer for years at his company. He wasn't satisfied with those results and his company contracted with our company to help him go from being an A player to an A+ player. He wanted to go from qualifying for the Master's tournament to winning the Master's. This is exactly the mentality Rick had. So they invested in him. Rick had spent years in his car driving to meetings with potential clients. Rick knew everything about giving effort. If there was a project in his territory, he would get pulled in. He had done a masterful job of connecting with potential clients in his territory well before they were considering a project. Rick knew virtually every president in his territory in the niche market they served. Better yet, those presidents knew and valued Rick.

John Maxwell says, "If you want to go up, you have to give up." Rick knew all about giving up as he invested years connecting with people. Average reps don't want to give up anything to be successful. Since we started working with Rick, he has sold over 300% of quota every year.

Each of us, when we were first dating our spouse or partner, probably gave effort in showing ways to impress him or her. We would buy gifts. We would spend time talking. We would do other things in an effort to connect at a new level. Unfortunately, many times after we got married those efforts ceased or, at least, were minimized. Effort is needed to be sustainable.

3. Be Human

Lastly, if you want to connect with people you have to be human with them. Some may call it down-to-earth. Others would say vulnerable. Remember, there is a human on the other side of the table who has real goals, fears, and ideals impacting the decision to act. Being "human" is one of the hardest things for some sales reps and managers to do. They show up prepared and they get down to business.

One of the best sales managers I ever had was a guy name Steve. Steve had this way of encouraging people that instilled a belief into their own abilities. I took Steve on a call to Austin, Texas to meet with the executive team of company who was looking at our software. The meeting went well and when we left, Steve shared his thoughts on many of the great things I had done in the meeting. When I asked him what I could have done better, he said I could have been more conversational and less strictly business. A few more times I took him on calls, he would say the same thing. It took me a while to understand that being human first is the key to being a great conversationalist. When I shared my "value introduction" and then for some reason shared that it was my first day on the job with Sandy, I was being human with her. Most reps would probably say, why would you ever say that? Don't you believe that no one wants to work with a new, inexperienced rep? My vulnerability put her in a place where she was able to open up. Remember, she went from being procurement-like to sharing her history and personal story with me.

I was working with a sales manager on the West Coast. He had been successful for many years as a sales rep and was promoted to VP of Sales. I had been working with his team for a while and they were constantly telling me about how much of a jerk he was. Yet, I would meet with the VP and based upon the sales reps' portrayals I was expecting him to sound and behave differently. He shared how his reps were not following his direction. He was located on the West Coast and his reps were spread out across the Western United States. I asked him how many times he had visited the reps in their town and spent time getting to know them. Had he even taken the time to invest in them and to connect with them? His answer was "no." So many managers sit in their offices, pointing towards the directions they want their team to go, without taking the time to connect. The VP visited each rep, spending forty-eight hours discussing strategy, doing something fun, and just getting to know each of them. He shared stories about his background and listened to each of his rep's stories and experiences. It was amazing how that broke down the walls each felt toward the other.

Once we get human with someone, find a commonality, and share some stories we can relate to, we find a connection and a bond begins to form. There is something that happens to the emotions when there is a connection in our personal lives and in our professional lives. This is not a friendship bond, but instead a bond of trust and rapport.

Unfortunately, the very next year, we were having the same conversation. He had not spent any real face-to-face or one-on-one time connecting after that first meeting nearly a year earlier. Connecting with someone is not "one and done." Again, we can compare it to the dating example; we must keep effort into play. Are you truly invested in them or are you temporarily trying to pick them up? You know, like a guy in a bar throwing pick up lines to meet women? When you are truly vested in the other side, they will recognize the need to develop the connection you have.

Old Thinking: "Get them to be my friend and they will buy from me."

New Thinking: "Connect with them and I will have more meaningful conversation to figure out if I can help."

Reflection for the Sales Representative

1. What is my intent as I engage at the beginning of every new relationship? Am I truly investing in them or am I trying to pick them up or manipulate them into liking to me so they will buy from me?
2. Ask your sales manager to attend your meeting so he can see if you are being conversational or getting down to business too quickly. Or maybe your focus is too much on backslapping, football, or fishing. The sales manager should know and be able to provide an honest evaluation.
3. When and where are you the best at conversations in your life? What's different there as compared to where you are the least likely to be conversational? How can you bridge the gap into your business conversations?
4. What are new ways you can give effort to connecting with the people with whom you engage?
5. How can you connect with the others in your organization that you rely on to support you in your efforts?

Reflection for the Sales Manager

1. So many times as sales managers, we love going out and visiting the clients with our reps and building relationships and connections, but we fail to put effort

into our connections and relationships with our reps. Evaluate yourself on whether or not you have invested into a connection with each rep. What can you do to enhance those connections?

2. How can you connect with other leaders in the organization that have teams that support your reps?

3. In your defined sales process, is connecting stage one of your sales process?

CHAPTER 8

CREATING YOUR YELLOW BRICK ROAD

As a kid growing up in the country, we only got three TV channels. Cable TV had not made it out that far with the plethora of channels most households are used to having today. Good television was hard to come by but *The Wizard of Oz* was an annual family affair in our household. We looked forward to it each year because it was something we could all watch together.

Most people probably know the story. Dorothy was a young lady who made her way to the land of Oz where she was trapped due to a tornado that relocated her house. She wanted to go back home to Kansas, but this fairytale place didn't have the same logic of the "real world." She was instructed by the "good witch" to meet with the great and mighty Oz who could help her go home. Not knowing where she was or where she was going, Dorothy asked how to get there. There was only one way. Dorothy had to follow the yellow brick road. How perfect? There was a bright yellow road that clearly outlined the journey she must tread to get to where she needed to go.

Wouldn't it be nice if there were a yellow brick road you could follow to get you and your client to the desired outcome? While there won't be any manifestations of yellow bricks for you to follow on your journey together, you can have a process that enables you to guide your client and yourself. After all, if you don't know what your process is, how can you get the client to understand the value of it?

Imagine you receive a knock on your door. You open it and a complete stranger is standing there and says, "Follow me! It's important!"

The man takes off running up the street. Are you following him or are you asking questions and staying put until you hear more? Now, imagine for a moment the scenario changes. The man knocks and when you answer, he screams, "I need help saving a child's life!"

Are you following him now? You are probably passing him as he runs. The odds are much higher you will follow him now because you understand the value of your effort. Even with your good intentions, if the client doesn't understand the value the next step will have, he probably won't agree to it or follow you.

I've heard sales reps tell their clients, "Here is what I need the next steps to be. Here is what I think we should do as the next step."

You may be saying something similar, trying to be "consultative" in your approach because you are trying to get to the decision-maker. So, you tell the client something like, "I really need to sit down with your boss and understand her goals, strategies and plans, so I can figure out if I can help your organization."

At this point, the rep wonders why the client doesn't agree or resists this process. Again, our purpose is to help them.

- *The rep says:* "I think, I feel, I want, and I need." You are not enriching but rather you are being salesy and not consultative.

- *The rep says:* "You should…" You are not enriching because you are just being bossy.
- *The rep says:* "What my clients found to be helpful as a next step is…and this is why…" You are not selling to the client, you are consulting the client and enriching them with helpful information.

"Everyone wants to learn but no one wants to be taught."

Think about teenagers. When you try to tell them what to do, they push back. Selling works the same way. Many times, as the prospect is trying to do things correctly, she doesn't need a pushy sales guy trying to convince her to buy his product so he can get paid. Remember the story of Mike in the first chapter? As reps, we may say "We are here to help you," but then we tell them "What I want, I need, and I think…"

This is why you can't just say it! Your words and actions will ultimately give you up. Your intent has to be real and you have to share the value from your previous client's point of view to have influence.

Remember, your client's process isn't there to annoy you. Clients have a process for procuring the solutions or services they seek. Many times the process has already been defined. Some are more formal than others. Some clients don't have a process and they are trying to figure it out as they go. I see so many reps take the client's buying process personally, as if the client is actually trying to tick off the rep.

Brent Henderson, a top speaker and author says it best when he says you have to seek to understand before being understood. Understand their process and then share with them what process your most successful clients have used and what value it brought them. Be clear about how that process helped your successful clients and better enabled you to assist them. Then share how blending that process into theirs may help.

Too often, we want clients to do everything we ask them to do (blindly), but the reality is that they have, more than likely, been over-promised and under-delivered by others. They are skeptical and are trying to protect their time, their boss's time (who probably assigned them this project), and trying to do their best for their company. Maybe they resist because they work for an organization that has a strict buying process. Sometimes you just can't get around their process. If you find yourself in those situations, you will have to make a gut call as to whether or not you can make an impact using their process. Blind Request for Proposals with defined demo scripts from procurement or a consultant are great examples of where we are sometimes limited in our ability to influence the process. Trust your gut in these situations and work with your sales management team in determining how to handle these potential time-wasters.

It could be true that if the client doesn't modify their process, you can't truly help them any more than to tell them you can't help them. It would be a complete waste of your time and theirs to proceed. Sometimes the best you can say is "I am not sure I can help you," but in walking away you can still educate.

The rep says, "The clients I have helped in the past have told me the real help came when we did (whatever the next step is). They told me that by going through that process it helped them (however it helped them)."

Wait a moment and then clarify by asking, "Am I correct that you don't see any value in that type of help?"

If they do, more than likely they become flexible and if they don't, then you probably can't help them. Remember, we can't help everyone. Some clients' cultures just don't align with yours.

It is up to you to define your yellow brick road. What's your process for handling blind RFP's and determining whether or not you are going to respond? What's your process for handling requests for references early in the process? What's your process for an inbound lead? What's your process when a previous client calls back? What's your ideal client's buying process and why? If you don't know, we, more often than not, follow the client's process. When we blindly follow the client's process, more often than not, we get commoditized (as we talked about in the previous chapter). We can't help when we get commoditized.

John Maxwell shared with me that rarely does anything great come from aimlessly wandering as compared with intentionally doing something. When we have purpose for what we are doing and can share "value stories" from our client's point of view, we increase our odds of enriching them and experiencing success.

Imagine driving up to a guy at stop light and honking to get his attention so you can say, "Hey, I am lost and I don't know how to get to the airport."

He responds, "Go ahead. Start driving and I'll follow you to get there."

Someone following the lost can't do anything but waste two people's time. That's what happens when we don't know where we are going and just follow the client's process.

Next, let's learn about the key to defining your sales process. I am not talking about the stages in your sales process built into your CRM system. I am talking about the actions you follow in all the scenarios you encounter. Here are some steps to help you get stated in one scenario, but it's up to you to define the rest or to work with a company like mine that will help you:

- List all the ways you encounter new leads or prospects. Web lead, voicemail call-in lead, RFP from a source you know, blind RFPs, and client referral. List them all.
- Now, what would be your ideal process for following up and for your first conversation? Do you reach out to schedule a first-call via email or phone? Do you do both? What's the email look like? I use the same email or voicemail message every time, because it's the process I've defined and it has proven to work for me and my clients. If you don't take the time to define it, than you're winging it. Winners don't wing it. Peyton Manning didn't win all those games in the NFL by showing up and winging it. No, he was intentional with a game plan and worked with his players to perfect the plan in practice so that when the game was played the team just executed. Be a pro and prepare, so you can lead. If you wing this, you will wing it somewhere else. If you take shortcuts, you will be prone to taking shortcuts.

My clients have heard me say this hundreds of times: "Where you behave someway in one place in your life, it will show up in other places in your life." So if you wing it, you will be prone to winging it. Winging it is not being intentional.

- Do you go ahead and have the first detailed conversation with the client if you get them on the phone right away, or do you schedule them to do that call? It matters!

I have a defined process for just about every scenario I encounter and have a process for even when I encounter things that are new. I have a process for how to handle RFP's. When I worked for Bluelock, I used to get RFP's and I would put them through my initial process. Some I would keep based upon the interactions in that process. Others, I would email out to other reps and say, "Here is an RFP and I am not going to work it because I don't think I can help them, but if you would like it and would like to run with it, let me know."

From time to time, someone would raise a hand and start chasing that rabbit. Not one single time did another rep ever win a project I passed on. My process helped me figure out if I was setup for success to help them. I've been on the client's side and I've had to read RFP's. Who wants to read a hundred page RFP response from a vendor who can't help you?

The reality is that one of the biggest values I bring my clients is a process that helps them be successful. Our value is not in what we say, it's in what we do and what our clients say about what we do for them.

My ability to articulate a process that has helped my best clients and then execute it, is a clear "value" I bring to all my clients and one of the biggest reasons they continue to do business with me. I hear them refer to the clarity of the process and level of engagement they encountered with me and my engagement team who supported me in the sales process. They talk about how we covered things no one else did. They talk about the fact that my process uncovered something they had not considered. I've heard how the process gave them validation they would be treated right even after signing the contract. I setup my process to help me help my clients and I am very clear about setting the expectations for that. Helping your clients with the buying process is "thought leadership." Help them to be successful in this project and they will never forget you. Again, we can only help those who align with our value. If they don't value you or your process, they usually won't buy from you.

Old Thinking: *"I am good. I can show up and perform."*

New Thinking: *"I owe it to my client and team to be prepared. I can't lead, if I don't know where I am going."*

Reflection for the Sales Representative

1. Do you have a play book (defined-process) or do you wing it? I personally feel those who consistently don't "wing it" will outperform the more naturally-talented sales rep. A prepared person who constantly works at it will eventually outgrow an unprepared more talented person who caps out on talent only.

2. Do you find that people are pretty good at aligning with your process or is it a constant struggle? If you do, you are not alone and should know that it's normal. You can work to change that. What are your "intent words," and what value is there for your clients to follow you?

3. From time to time, you are going to be asked by your boss to chase a rabbit you don't think you can catch. Seek to understand before being understood. Have the tough conversation with your manager. There may be logic that makes sense in this instance. If your sales manager constantly gives you bad advice and forces you to follow it, you may need to move on. Or you may need to get better at influencing him and helping him understand your process and why it helps your organization by following it. Remember,

managers and bosses are human too and they are not trying to punish you or waste your time. They are trying to win. Trust your instincts, but sometimes you just have to do what you are told to do.

Reflection for the Sales Manager

1. Work with your team to define the "sales process." You can tell if they are winging it. Be prepared to share what process is working for other reps. Be slow to force them to follow a process just because you said so. Share stories and examples of how it helped you or other reps and try to influence the thinking. Remember, if we don't change the way they think, their actions won't naturally follow and you will be telling them again and again what to do. While there is a science aspect of sales, in actuality, sales is an art. Don't give them the words, help them think through the science of the process. I know *you* are in a hurry for change. Don't shortcut the process or it will create the hard way. Clearly, if someone on your team is struggling, you must either replace, reposition, or invest in some sales coaches who can help from a safe place. My experience is that people who appear to be "uncoachable" usually don't feel safe enough to be vulnerable. Everyone I have ever been asked to work with who was labeled "uncoachable" ended up being very coachable.

2. Unifying your team is a huge goal. I encourage you to concentrate on the beliefs you want them focused on. If you aren't careful, putting guys who don't get it, in with guys who do, can frustrate both sides. This is why we sometimes coach and mentor one-on-one on these subjects. I would not suggest working the team to have a unified process but again unified in the beliefs and behaviors. This is an art. What works for

one rep may not work for another. Ask your reps in one-on-one meetings what they think the process should be for a given situation? Don't test them. Testing destroys trust. Help them discover the process that works for them. Hold them accountable to figure it out and ask great questions.

CHAPTER 9

MAKE A DIFFERENCE EARLY

As I was interviewing for a job with a banking technology company, Ross, the Executive Vice President of Sales, asked me what I thought the biggest weakness was in my sales philosophy. After thinking about it, I shared the fact that I have probably bailed out of a few deals I may have been able to win.

When he asked me to explain, I told him that I only work on deals where I know I have a 75% chance or better at being successful. If, after the first conversation, I don't see alignment with them and the niche where I am successful, I usually bail. I've been told by many that I am walking away from deals I could have won, but I don't waste my time chasing rabbits I can't catch. I won't chase fifty bad deals to land a couple. I've learned over the years that by the end of the first or second meeting, I can tell whether or not I have a 75% chance or better of helping that particular client with their project. Ross didn't see that as a negative.

Over the years, I've won my fair share of projects and I've taken the time to talk with my clients. I've intentionally asked them, when did you believe I was the right person or our company was the right one to help you and your specific need? More often than not, they knew they wanted to work with me after our first conversation.

One day, I received an RFP from a major-name foundation out of New York. I had no previous experience with them. In my first conversation with the consultant, I followed my normal process for handling blind RFPs. I used my "first call process" to drive a business conversation. Two months later when they told me they had awarded us the contract, he shared that after that first meeting, he walked into the CIO's office and told him he believed he had found the "right" company to work with. That was before we even responded to the RFP. He told me everything we did after that just validated what he already thought. I had the privilege to work with a major law firm out of St. Louis, Missouri that employs some of the best people I have ever worked with. They told me they sent RFP's to sixty different companies before meeting with us. I decided to work on the project after my first conversation with the consultant, and because it was referred to us by a trusted partner. We showed up to the first meeting at the law firm to see at least twenty different IT leaders and respected influencers waiting to hear what we had to share. I remember the CIO kicking off the meeting by telling us not to try to sell to her, that it would be the decision of her team who would determine if they wanted to move forward with us. At the end of that first meeting, the CIO stood up and said, "I have not talked to my team yet, but I have no doubt you guys will be back for more conversation."

When we were told they were moving forward with us, their project manager shared that they felt like we were the right company from the first meeting. Everything we did from that point forward just validated their initial thoughts.

This pattern has repeated itself so much over the years that I could write pages and pages on these types of stories. What became apparent to me is that if I didn't connect, influence, and help in that first meeting, we might as well stop the process. More often than not, emotional decisions are made early. I find that when I win, I win early. Now you can lose the deal late, too. I have lost late due to unforetold circumstances: the "champion" died, the business was acquired, we couldn't reach agreement on terms of the contract, I missed something early in the process that I should not have missed, and more. But the reality is, that if I didn't win early, I didn't win.

In an earlier chapter, we discussed the ideal client. To win early, you must know the strategies and cultures of the businesses within the niche where you are currently successful. There will be aspects you learn that will also help you in that initial conversation as you truly begin to understand your ideal client.

Over the years of working with reps, there are two common approaches to the first meetings. Most sales people take one or both approaches as part of their first conversation. They either try to give a PowerPoint presentation about the company (you know that marketing-defined sales presentation that says why you are the world's greatest at doing whatever you do) or they show up asking questions (you know the meeting, where you ask questions about their goals, strategies, and concerns). They do this in the hopes they can uncover the secret formula enabling them to magically sell to the potential client. While the first method may meet exactly what the client is asking for, it also goes back to our commoditization conversation. The faster you talk about your company and products, the faster you get commoditized. You can't help the client and make a difference, if you commoditize yourself.

In the second approach, the rep wonders why executive management doesn't want to sit down with him to have this conversation about goals and challenges. Over the years, "consultative selling" has been communicated to the sales industry as the differentiated approach to being successful. Consultative selling is where you show up and ask them questions about their goals and pains and share how you can help with those. While that is better than option one, in today's sales industry, a significant amount of sales people are doing this exact same thing. When you act and sound like everyone else, you get commoditized. This is why more companies are sending RFPs. I am showing you a methodology that will enable you to beat the best consultative sales people in the market.

Once when I was working with a group of reps, we had planned a role-play session. One of the sales VPs was frustrated with my teachings, because it went against what he believed. So, this VP wanted to prove me wrong. I thought it could be an interesting learning experience. He said he wanted to role-play his approach and then have me role-play my approach. We didn't want to turn this into some type of competition; it was to show two approaches and then let the group provide feedback. I came up with the scenarios we role-played in front of his peers and their reps. I actually called in a guy from our company to play the role of the client as we have helped many clients hold role-play sessions. He did a great job of playing exactly how the traditional consultative sales person would behave. He asked a good number of questions and did 80% of the talking, as you would hope would happen. A good rep talks 20% and listens 80%. He did a great job with that. Then, we did the exact same scenario, but I used the approach I am going to share with you.

At the end of the role-plays, the VP and I asked questions of the group about the two approaches and what they observed as differences in the approaches. Here was the gist of the consensus. Neither approach talked about our company or our products. Both approaches did a decent job of discovering the goals and details of the project, but only the approach I used, brought "thought leadership" and left the "client" with a sense of confidence that I could really help. It was overwhelmingly believed that the first approach was heavily valued for the rep only, whereas the second approach was as equally valuable for the rep as it was the client.

If the client doesn't walk away from this first meeting getting value out of the meeting, they are not going to meet with you again. That is, unless they like to waste their time. Over the years, this idea of showing up and asking questions has caused more RFP's to be built, just to avoid being cornered in a room with each vendor's rep answering the same questions.

Want to know where a good number of my leads came from over the early days of sales training and coaching? My wife, a CIO at the time, who would have meetings with vendors and would hand them my card because of how bad their sales process was. The "art of discovery" and "thought leadership" and helping is so key during this first conversation.

Remember, there are two ways we can help our clients. The first, we help them by enriching them around their strategy and pre-buying process to assure a successful decision for them. Second, we can sell them a solution that helps enable that strategy. If you don't enrich on the first one, more often than not, we don't get to help on the second. The "thought leadership" that comes from knowing our ideal client is the yellow brick road to helping with the first conversation.

I agree with trying to get the client to talk first, but in today's market, businessmen aren't interested in wasting time answering your questions. Sometimes the client will want you to talk first, so they may ask you to share about your company. Don't panic or use bad practice. Most of all, don't become one of those controlling sales reps who acts as if he has just been asked to do something illegal, making the conversation awkward. This goes back to Chapter Eight and knowing your process. How do you handle it, when you have to go first?

I usually say, "The best way to tell you about us is to share with you the success my clients have experienced in the niche we have created. There are some common trends around their strategies, culture, and beliefs and how they have aligned with that niche. Why don't we talk through these and your situation and figure out if there is any alignment between the two?" I've never *not* had anyone agree to this.

We previously covered your ability to map out the strategies and cultures in your ideal client. I am not going to map out everything we cover in our full training engagements because it could be a book by itself. If you fully want to be great at "the art of discovery and thought leadership," you have to be an expert in the following four areas in your field. The diagram depicts the four areas that will guide you in helping the client in their pre-buying success.

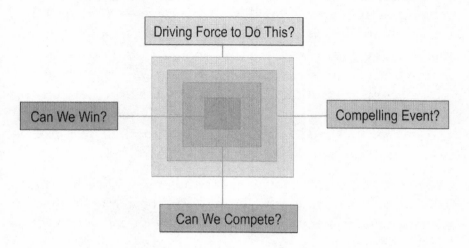

You will notice the center of the square depicts how there is a step-by-step process to figuring out if this project will happen at all, happen now, and if we have a real shot at being included. I talk to reps all the time and the first conversation feels like some awkward line dance that you have never seen before. This outline will give you the ability to educate, challenge, and lead your client in that first meaningful conversation.

Let's break down each section and what it means:

A. *Driving Force* is the energy behind any project

Most reps don't understand driving force and tend to focus on compelling events (which is the reason to act now). But without Driving Force, no project happens. A freshman football player really wants to make varsity. He believes if he is the starting quarterback for four years in high school, he will be recruited by a great college. He wants to be a professional football player some day and he has laid out a path to get himself there. With the season six months away, he sees he is behind other players during off season workouts. He starts working out harder, putting in extra reps and studying the playbook with coaches after practice. The driving force is his desire to be a professional football player some day. The compelling event to act now is that he sees he is behind other players with only 6 months before the season. If he didn't have the driving force of playing varsity so that he could get recruited by a college with a track record of producing professional football players, he probably would not do the extra work.

There are different reasons why someone may be willing to talk about your product for a potential project. Great sales reps can, not only tell the difference between issues that lead to no project verses those that actually cause people to make things happen.

The following are the three types of forces we encounter and it is often up to us to help them navigate from one tier to the other for the project to become important enough to move forward. It is our ability to help validate, navigate or lead the client from one issue tier to the other that will often determine if they get value in the first conversation. Remember, most people wake up every day doubting their value and abilities to succeed. Our intent is to help the client succeed and not to just sell them our product/company. By helping the client understand "driving force," both of us succeed. While without driving force, we are both wasting our time.

- Curiosity Forces –Interesting and may drive them to be willing to meet and do exploration. They may even ask you for a proposal but they go silent after showing much interest and saying the right things.
- Important Forces – Significant enough to warrant a detail evaluation but a change may not come about as

distractions keep them from making it a priority to get it done with intentionality.

- Driving Forces – once it is recognized that the impact of not doing something creates so much risk or results in a lost opportunity that the client has motivation to act.

B. *Compelling Event* is why they act now

This is the event that causes the driving force to have meaning NOW. A project with driving force and without a compelling event runs the risk of lasting a long time before it comes to closure or never happening even though it was important to the topic of discussion. This is one of those projects that was supposed to be done in six months but ended up taking two years to come about. It wasn't until something compelling happened to cause them to act on the purchase or change.

As the rep, we have to understand if there is a compelling event, so we can set correct expectations internally about the project. But we can also help the client understand the risk of doing all this research and not acting, if there is not a compelling event. What business professional intentionally wants to invest hours, days, weeks or even months into research, only to be patted on the head and sent back to the office being rejected by someone who didn't see enough compelling reason to act now? We have all worked with clients who were told at the time of approval that the idea was good and that they should do it, but not now, due to other priorities. Understanding the reasons and details of why this happens is vital to helping your prospect avoid failure. Our job is not to create a compelling event but instead help them understand the importance of it, what that type of event looks like, and help them create awareness in the organization if they are going to carry this forward for success. This will enable support to shift from an *important issue* to a *compelling issue* and the need to act now. A compelling reason doesn't have to be anything more than the right executive, who also has the authority to approve all expenditures, setting a deadline for the project to be completed.

An additional example of how *driving force* and *compelling event* work together can be seen in the following story:

A few years ago, I decided to lose weight and start working out and eating right six days a week. The driving force behind that change was a planned trip to Cabo, Mexico and *I didn't want to be the fat guy on the beach.* It wasn't until I scheduled the flight that the driving force to not being fat on the beach became compelling enough to take action and see it through. Based on my definition of being fat, I knew I only had six months to get there and the purchasing of the flight made it a compelling event to act now. What if I didn't care about being fat on the beach? What if I knew I had plenty of time to lose weight and didn't need to act now? In the same way, a CIO may see a need for a new disaster recovery plan and it keeps her up at night. It's an important issue for sure. An outage could cost the company millions. But without a compelling issue or event, the company more than likely won't agree to spending 2x the current minimal plan already in place. It's not until a top client threatens to leave because of a lack of a DR plan that the company decides to invest in the upgraded project. The driving force behind the project is that they need to keep their clients and existing revenue. The compelling event is that a major client is going to leave if they don't pass the IT Audit around their disaster recovery plan.

C. Can We *Compete?*

What fighter would get into the ring with another boxer where he has no shot of winning *and* only gets paid if he wins? Only a desperate fighter. Desperate people are usually self-serving and in survival mode. This type of person usually makes their situation worse over time. Therefore, we need to fully understand the circumstances keeping us from being considered a serious contender. Understanding the history of the project, previous project reviews in your current position and at previous jobs, experience with other vendors, and how they learned about us, are for the most part cultural experiences that have created beliefs. Some of those experiences might limit the client's ability to consider us. It is the adoption of those beliefs that many times determine if you are really going to be taken seriously no matter what your process or value looks like. It's those beliefs that determine what they share with you, what process they use, and how they respond to your recommendations based on previous successes and failures.

It's when we are detached from the outcome and are not desperate, that we can share with the client. We can share how or why we can or can't help based upon behavior we have seen from the clients we have previously helped. It's not until we challenge their beliefs can we see if there is alignment in beliefs.

For example, a client who values price over client experience will usually try to use a process that minimize the experience. This will limit your ability to compete because they won't experience a difference with you from the beginning. Even if they did, it usually doesn't make a difference. Sometimes through education and the ability to help them understand why your previous clients cared about experience over price that you are able to influence them. It isn't our job to just say the words but to validate whether those words resonate or not. The challenge is that no one is going to say, "I don't value great client services."

Everyone wants it, but not everyone is willing to pay for it. Maybe they have experience with a certain vendor from their previous job where they implemented that solution and it made a huge difference for them. They loved it. They are now looking at this company and your company. They want to compare the two. The question is whether or not you can compete. Are they already emotionally tied to that company? Those emotional ties can deny you the opportunity of allowing them to experience the value you bring.

We can't help them if they are not willing to pay for the experience. We can only help those who are willing to pay us for the experience.

D. Can We *Win?*

You can only win when decision-makers share goals aligned with your key values and sound like the clients with whom you've successfully dealt in the past. When they start repeating your words back to you, articulating what they expect to experience partnering with you, you can win. If you don't hear the "value" words you would typically hear from your successful clients, don't be afraid to explain why those values were important to previous clients. Maybe they don't care or maybe they don't know to care. Remember, if they don't understand the value in it for them, they won't engage in the process. Help them learn and if these things are important, you will see the alignment. If you don't think you can win, you won't.

Each time you move up the ladder to a higher person on the decision/approval tree, this process must be repeated.

Alignment with a project manager doesn't mean you have alignment with the decision- maker or the project-initiator.

In our consulting, training, and coaching clients, we work with each rep to develop his ability to master these first conversations and determine with whom they can be successful. If you only work on deals you can win (maybe you won't, but you can), then your time is not wasted chasing those proverbial rabbits you can't catch. In these conversations, you are setting the stage for what they will experience. If they value this type of experience, they will begin an emotion process of selecting you. It doesn't mean it's your deal yet. It means they are beginning to lean your direction. It's in how you continue to validate that experience that will increase your odds of helping.

Old Thinking: "If I show up and ask a bunch of questions, I am being consultative."

New Thinking: "I can help them learn by leveraging my stories about the niche we succeed in to frame my questions so they get value from the thought experience."

Reflection for the Sales Representative

1. Do you understand what the driving forces were that pushed your clients into making a change? If you can understand what drove your existing clients to make a change, this will enable you to tell the difference between *important issues* and *compelling issues*. Most reps trivialize this portion. They want to be more efficient and more compliant. Add this to your client interview processes we discussed in previous

chapters to further understand the driving force behind the strategies.

2. You may not be able to have this conversation on your own. Your ability to leverage your teammates who have different skill sets for storytelling, consulting, or sharing client experiences can aid you in making an impact on the life of the person on the other side of the conversation. I've had clients tell me that what they experienced in the first conversation made the difference. You are the quarterback, it's your job to call the play and set the team in motion. Do you know who to leverage and can you explain the goal of the first conversation? This isn't a technical conversation. This is about strategic and culture alignment. Some teammates may struggle as they want to jump to "product," because its easier than having consultative conversations. Share this book with them, sit down, and work with them prepping for the meeting. How do you know when to pull others into this conversation and when to go alone?

3. Do you use buzzwords in your slides and your conversations? We are "a world class leader in the XYZ space!" "Our robust solution allows us to make our clients more profitable." "We have white glove service that enables our clients to have a powerful experience with our company." Those types of marketing words might be okay in your marketing materials, but they are being used by everyone. The more you use these words, the more you will struggle to connect. Where are you using buzzwords and why?

Reflection for the Sales Manager

1. Not everyone will have this conversation the same way, but you can set the tone for the culture and the beliefs that your team will operate under for these

discussions. How can you work with your team to understand the driving force reasons behind why your clients are making changes and buying from you? Same questions can be made in compelling events, ideal client characteristics, sales process, etc.

2. John Maxwell has a book called *Great Leaders ask Great Questions*. It's during the process of helping your reps think, versus when you give direction, that can make a difference in developing your team and its culture. Sometimes, it feels like you have to tell your team how to go to the bathroom. It's so tempting to give direction. It's in those moments where great leaders learn to ask better questions. I always wanted my team to go out and be creative and not being afraid of failing. Enable them through questions. Give them the freedom to take risks with no fear of ridicule from you. This type of conversation is hard. When it's mastered, you will find that your one-on-one sales meetings discussing their pipeline and opportunities will feel much more productive for both of you. You will be able to talk about *driving force*, *compelling event*, *ideal client characteristics*, *can you compete*, and *can you win*. When these meeting become more effective, growth happens. When growth happens in your reps, sales growth happens.

John Maxwell says, "If you want to grow your company, grow your people." How can you structure your one-on-one deal review conversations to enable growth, allowing the freedom to fail, and not just making this one more "directive" discussion?

CHAPTER 10

JOINT ENVISIONING WORKS!
JUST ASK YOUR DOCTOR

The art of compromise is something that, when perfected, can be as beautiful as a mountaintop sunrise. When you figure out how to make your vision work with your client's vision, you are on the road to finding so much more success within your career. I was consulting with a software company that was working on a project with a fast-growing prospect. The prospect was looking to replace their main large ERP application commonly used within their type of organization. My client's process looked like this:

1. Intro conversations
2. Business Discovery
3. Technical Discovery
4. Presentation
5. Proposal
6. Contracts

My client had met with different executives and worked through the discussions necessary to conduct business and technical discovery. They had spent at least twenty hours on site, interviewing and discovering challenges. When it came time to make the presentation, our client did their own company overview, full of the typical marketing slides, telling the bank executives everything they needed to know in order to believe our client was the greatest company.

Next, they proceeded to run through a six-hour demo that described their solution. The presentation was consistently trying to hit on the areas our client had discovered through interviews and conversations where the client believed it could make a difference. The prospect loved the demo and raved about it after the fact. The client told me they were confident after the presentation and left the meeting feeling it was their project to lose. Two weeks later, our client was eliminated. In the call, the prospect shared how our client's competitor came in and did a demo. The prospect liked the functionality of the competitor's software application better.

The client was devastated and reached out to me to see if my company could help them figure out how to prevent this situation from happening again.

I am not here to tell you that the above process won't work. It will work, sometimes. What I want to share with you is something that, in my experiences of working with many clients across multiple vertical markets, works nearly every time – with your ideal client.

Stories like the one above are so common in many sales organizations and it's this type of sales process that is holding many companies back. In this chapter, we are not talking about the "presentation" that you come up with for your meetings. In fact, imagine that there is no such thing as a "meeting" and instead, you are about to attend a *Joint-Envisioning Session*. It is called a joint-vision because it's not just the rep's vision of how this product will work. It's how the client and the rep can see the project working together. Traditionally, as the salesperson, you would have gathered all of this information through the discovery process and when it's time for the meeting, you show up and present your solution. The rep gets up and tap dances along with his dog and pony show, trying to persuade everyone to buy his product. That's the old way of doing things. It's time for a change. The one-directional approach is different than what I typically desired as a salesperson. If the client can't see themselves in the experience, then all they are doing is comparing products. Dog and pony shows don't have the emotional buy-in a joint-vision does.

A few years ago, I was looking to get bids to have my basement finished. The area was roughly 1500 square feet of unfinished space. I asked three companies to meet with me. The first company came in and showed me pictures of all of their basement projects. They had examples of all of the great things they could do for me. They had a great product and it was so impressive to see the finished projects. The salesman asked me about the type of basement I wanted and how I wanted to use the space. Next, he did a drawing of my unfinished basement. When he returned, he presented a design based on the features and functions I wanted. He was also referred to me by a friend who had a fantastic experience with the company.

The second company was brought in to give an estimate because I personally knew the guy who ran the company. He asked questions about what I wanted in my basement and walked through the basement to get my ideas. He explained his company's process and explained how his team would work with me on the project. He measured the basement and had his team build me a 3D video of the finished basement. It was like a virtual reality walking through the "finished" basement based upon their design. It was impressive!

The third company was recommended to me through word of mouth, thanks to another friend. I brought company three in to my basement. He asked me how I envisioned the space being used and why. After walking through the basement, he pointed out a few things that were going to be challenges for me in that plan. As an example, he shared how the windows that already existed were going to potentially limit my ability to count the space as bedroom space. He then explained how this might be remedied. I was frustrated with him. I asked him why neither of the other two guys brought this up and if he was sure about the building code? He then shared how we should consider a few other ideas that might help me use the space better. When he returned with his drawing, he suggested ways of using the space and options that would lower my expense but not kill the feel I was looking for. He took me into the basement and literally walked me through how this would work while including me in the process.

Each company had a great plan and great people. Which one did I select? Number three. Why? I selected him because he never really tried to impress me. He didn't try to be my friend. He took a joint- envisioned approach to find the right solution for the right investment. He also brought the most challenging parts of the project into light and helped me think through what I really wanted, what I needed, and what was going to work best. Neither of the other two guys brought up the windows and later, I asked them about it. They both knew it was going to be a challenge and said they were going to address it in the final drawing. Contractor three's ability to walk me through things honestly and talk about how it would work, laying out the pros and cons, got me emotionally tied to his approach. My trust factor with him was the highest. While all three asked me questions and returned with a solution, only one came back to jointly- envision how it would work. The others came back to present their solution to impress me and to get me to move forward.

Get this point! When someone is part of building the vision, gets emotionally tied, and cemented to the process, it becomes like a single lady who falls in love with the man who is bad news. By the time she is emotionally tied to him, logic goes out the window. Joint-envisioning gets the emotional buy-in by helping them think through the solutions for the difficult challenges that await them if they are not prepared.

This reminds me of a time when I was working with one of the nation's largest automotive dealers. They had talked to all of our competitors and shared with me that none of them were listening. Each salesperson was dictating to them what they thought they should do, but no one was listening to what they wanted to do. We listened to what they were trying to do and we shared a few similar clients' experiences during our first conversation. We knew they had some core beliefs or cultural beliefs, and that if those beliefs were not aligned with how we thought to help them, there would be emotional rejection of the idea. I am not telling you to just try to please your clients and their every whim. I *am* talking about recognizing the client's core beliefs and aligning your solution to those while also aligning to strategy and functional requirements. We met face-to-face. I held a whiteboard session and we walked through the detailed agenda that I'd developed. We talked about options and the pros and cons of each based on our successes and failures with clients. The automotive company was a part of the solution process as we made recommendations based upon what they said. They never wavered in their belief that we were the right answer and agreed to pay 25% more for our solution over the nearest competitor.

For some reason, in business, we often fail to get that emotional buy-in because our desire to show up, demo our product, and do a presentation is more important. We believe that if only they see our product, watch the demo, and learn our features, functions, and benefits, they will fall in love and sign a purchase order. That approach can work, sometimes. But my sales clients don't want to rely on a hope strategy. They want a defined approach that clearly tells them and the client whether or not they are the right company to help them. Nine out of ten times when there is obviously alignment in values and needs, we know by the time we adjourn they want to move forward with us.

I am not telling you to follow this prescriptive approach like a recipe. I *am* trying to get you to begin to develop a process where you are not just showing up and throwing up, but tailoring your approach to the specific client, enabling them to be as emotionally tied to the solution as you are, assuring them you can help. I often call this a "working whiteboard session" where we cross our t's and dot our i's.

For a *Joint-Envisioning Session* to be effective, there are a few things that need to happen. There are five key steps towards building a joint-envision. If you follow these steps, you will give yourself the best chance to get emotional buy-in to a joint-vision.

1. Understand the current situation

We covered the "first conversations" earlier in the book. You must understand enough about the prospective client's situation to know if there are any show stoppers that would keep you from being able to successfully help them. You must know enough to have a feel for about 60-70% of the details that would be needed to solution the final product. You don't need to understand 100% of the discovery. It's okay if you do know it, but it's actually not ideal, because it means you are spending too much time in discovery, possibly slowing down the process, or making the process too hard. When selling, we want to cross every t and dot every i. But doing it too early can make the process feel too hard for the client *and* it can cause you to feel less helpful and more complicated and painful. We can't help those that feel we are being too difficult. In my basement story, all three companies did this step. The problem was that the first two contractors tried to understand everything and come back and present a final solution, looking for buy-in. The winning company understood enough to come back and talk through concepts and challenges so that we could figure them out together.

2. 50% Technical fit and 50% Cultural Fit

We've covered technical fit. Now you have to understand the cultural beliefs as well. I was recently working with a Canadian company who was not interested in a particular piece of software to be used as part of the solution we presented to them. This software is what we recommended 90% of the time to our clients, because it works extremely well. Their reasoning was based on a previous experience with that software company leaving them completely dissatisfied. That software solution would have been a great technical fit, but culturally it didn't align. Culture is based on their beliefs and behaviors. In this case we were trying to align our client's experience with our approach to doing business. But their experiences were not our experiences. Their culture expectations were different. Most sales people never think about this and it's a mistake.

While we have to make sure the solution is a culture fit for the client, in the same fashion, I must also make sure our two companies can work together. Companies spend more time hiring an employee and making sure they are a good technical/aptitude/cultural fit than they do when they are choosing the companies they work/partner with in projects. We want to focus more on aptitude and their product set and less on how our two companies will actually work together. More projects fail for cultural reasons than technical reasons!

I had a friend in college who was always able to date the most beautiful ladies. There was this one woman he had dated for six months. She was super smart, beautiful, and always very conversational when we were in social settings. One day, he told me he broke it off with her. I asked why and he said there were just too many cultural differences in their religious, financial, and political beliefs. It didn't matter how pretty she was, he understood the importance of the cultural fit. In the same way, we must make sure our clients are thinking about cultural fit. To align cultures, we have to understand each of the cultures first.

3. Alignment on Who, What, and When

Once you have the technical and cultural information gathered, you schedule the joint-envisioning session with the people whose opinions and votes matter. This is done just like you normally would in the old way of presenting your company and products/solutions. If you don't have the decision-maker present, then you are, more than likely, wasting your time. Our goal is to have all the people who are influencing and deciding to be on the same page at the conclusion of this meeting.

Build an agenda with the client, explaining to them what you will be jointly covering and why and what you need them to bring to augment the discussion. This could include reports, drawings, or even a specific expert from their team. The goal is to talk, not just the technical aspects of the project, but also things like "change management," "cultural buying," and your "approach and vision" of what could be accomplished. Again, you do not want to show up and say here is exactly what you need to do. Instead, discuss a few options based on what you heard, talking through the pros and cons, advising based on your experience which approach fits technically, strategically, and culturally to the client's organization.

This is where you can talk through the really challenging technical parts and bring to life the issues that can cause failure. Talking through this with the decision-maker and the expert brings to life your experience by helping them get through this, but also raises the awareness of these types of challenges to the decision-maker. I guarantee, more often than not, they had no idea these challenges existed. By the client experiencing you bringing these challenges and then watching you and their expert come to an agreement on an approach, brings emotional comfort. So, build your agenda in a way that makes it possible for you to bring these things to light. Now, you should know slightly enough about this from discovery to know the options in which you might be successful. By sharing the pros and cons of each approach while making a recommendation based on the discussion, you will be so very helpful to their team. When we help, we build trust and with trust comes comfort. Comfort creates the emotional tie needed to get them as a new client. You can't fake this, so don't be superficial.

4. Define Success Criteria and Understand their Fears

Your process might go like this:

I like to start the meeting with a whiteboard session discussing these topics:

a) Write down the goals and strategies that you have learned and verify those to the targeting executives that may be new to the conversation. Add to the list.

b) What does success look like for you eighteen months from now? This enables the team to think through what is the most important measurement for success. You may have heard this from the project manager or some management level earlier. But the goal, if there is someone higher-level here for the first time, to gather this information.

c) What are your biggest concerns about the organization from a change management, cultural, or technical stand point? What are your concerns with the company at this point? Let's get those out there with a goal to address each one during the meeting. I find this to be helpful, especially if there are new decision-makers in the meeting for the first time. If you had part of this conversation before, then list what you heard and then add/verify/change as necessary. Recap so that problem areas come to life. We want everyone on the same page from the beginning of this meeting.

d) Now, what are your biggest concerns with the project? Most sales people only want to focus on making sure that what is being said sounds easy and that this is cut and dry. It's a mistake, because experience tells all buyers that things never go easy. Imagine the buyer is sitting there knowing this is a big project for the company and a make or break situation for her. Ninety-seven percent of all people fear failure. When you share your biggest concerns, you bring to life your ability to notice things that could crash the project but also how to address them. Think about how a medical doctor sits down with you and shares his concerns about the surgery you are considering. He brings them to light and then tells you his options and approaches for mitigating them. He includes you in the discussion while sharing his recommendation based on pros and cons. Trust levels rise significantly. He is helping you, the patient, with awareness and taking some ownership in choosing the outcome.

Our goal is to not make this simply a PowerPoint presentation (even though you will probably have some PowerPoint slides or a printed handout to present options or control the discussion). This is a discussion meeting or a working whiteboard session.

A recent study of 351 people proved a whiteboard session over a PowerPoint presentation was more successful. The participants were asked to imagine they worked at a company where they were responsible for improving the presentation skills of their sales staff. Participants were told they would be viewing a presentation regarding this topic and then were presented with a short, video about the "attention hammock," a phenomenon where, while listening to a spoken message, an audience's attention starts high, declines in the middle, and then peaks again at the end. However, the visuals accompanying the spoken message differed in using either PowerPoint, Zen, or whiteboard methods.

Participants who viewed the whiteboard approach found the presentation to be more credible and rated their presenter as being more experienced and trustworthy. Overall, the whiteboard presentation created an eight percent increase in perceived credibility compared to the other presentation methods.

In addition, by a margin of about 8%, participants in the whiteboard approach rated the presentation as clearer, easier to understand, and more enjoyable. Lastly, in a recall test at the end of the session, whiteboard participants were able to accurately remember significantly more message content than PowerPoint or Zen techniques. Most importantly, the whiteboard presentation generated an approximately 16% improvement in memory for message content – more than the numbers for both the PowerPoint and Zen combined.

If, during the whiteboard session, you connect with the client by hitting on every single item enabling success and overcoming concerns, you will, more than likely, gain emotional buy-in to the process. In the first conversation, you told them about the experience they were going to get working with you through your sales process, and now they are experiencing your help, firsthand.

This approach and communicated value will set you apart from the dog and pony show presentations or those approaches focused only on the product. I've said it a lot here and I am saying it again: this isn't about presenting the information as much as it is about leading them through a discussion and letting them be part of the decisioning process.

We were working with a client on the east coast. During the joint-envisioning discussion, we had whiteboarded their goals, success criteria, and concerns. We then discussed the technical details of their situation and what we had learned from our ealier discussions. This was our way of verifying the information we had gathered in the technical conversations, but this was also where we made sure we brought up specific difficult nuances of the project that they had not thought through or discussed with other vendors. As we shared stories of situations we saw in the market, we asked them to share their thoughts. We learned they hadn't thought through this aspect as much as they thought they had. This wasn't so much about the product and how we were going to serve it, but more about the specific technical challenges we needed to overcome by working together.

If you are in this situation, go to the whiteboard or have a conversation about it right then. We discussed the pros and cons to the options and helped them think through them. Then we were able to share with conviction what we would recommend based on their response. Their emotional tie to that solution became evident as they finally understood as a team what success looked like in their situation. Had we just presented to what they thought, we would have commoditized ourselves in the process. Instead, we were the only company that actually enriched their process through experience and expertise.

5. Educate and Validate

Once you get through the whiteboard session, you'll be ready to move on to the final part of the process. This is probably the real first session where we share who we are and what we do as it relates to serving clients similar to them. This can be in the same meeting or a different one. If you have the decision-makers present, you might as well move forward because you may not get them again. You know the information and now it is your job to help them understand how you are a strategic, technical, and cultural fit to work together. Have slides prepared and validate/add/change with them. At this point, we typically demo software and talk through our services specifically to address the goals and concerns. Do not do a canned presentation of how you are the best solution/company ever. Don't sell and convince, educate! You have earned trust; don't ruin it by being a dog in heat for the deal.

Don't be afraid to go to the whiteboard and explain how this is going to work. I remember a time when I was in Goodland, Kansas working on a project with a company. I was selling software that went across multiple functional areas of their business. I went to the whiteboard and drew out what we just discussed. I then demoed for thirty minutes, validating the key six things we discussed and sold a $750,000 project.

119

Obviously, I had other meetings before this, but I spent most of the time drawing out the process and less time showing blue and pink buttons in an application. If you sell services, it's not different. Whiteboard the process without getting mired down in details. The surgeon doesn't come in and show you scalpels, needles, and sutures when he explains the surgical approach. Don't do that either. Focus on the problem, the approach, and the outcome in a whiteboard discussion.

Finally, close the meeting by walking back through and validating how you addressed or didn't address the goals, success criteria, and concerns they shared earlier. If they don't validate how this was a different experience and share how this truly helped them, get out. You usually won't win. They didn't value it and/or you missed something earlier in the process that should have told you this. If this is the case, don't give them a proposal and hope it just works out. Address the red flag right there and express how this is different than your ideal client.

But if it did resonate and they share openly, take this blueprint you just built with them, and build a proposal that will help them align the value to the investment.

Old Thinking: Showing up and presenting our solution to their problem is the best way for me to convince them to buy.

New Thinking: If they are not part of the process of solving the problems and solutions, we run the risk of them not having an emotional tie to our approach and solution.

Reflection for the Sales Representative

1. You are responsible for making sure the team that is joining you in the client meeting is aligned and engaged to deliver with the right intent of this meeting. Prep with them and have a dry run, walk through of everything you have planned for your joint-envisioning session. Do not shortcut this. Be prepared. It only takes one "smart guy" on the other side of the table who jumps into some feature of your product they aren't going to love, to destroy the trust you started to build.

2. Be flexible! You may have to sometimes use powerpoint and other times a whiteboard. The important thing is to understand the setting where you will be meeting. Don't show up prepared for a whiteboard and then the potential client not have one. I typically expect a hybrid approach of PowerPoint and whiteboard to facilitate the conversation.

3. Customize and tailor every PowerPoint slide to what you are discussing with them, no matter how simple the project is. Don't go with a canned presentation. Canned presentations tell them they don't matter and that you are just pitching them like you do everyone.

4. This isn't a proposal meeting, but they will want to know pricing. Use the process!

Reflection for the Sales Manager:

1. Ask good questions about the meeting and the plan. You may even want to be a part of the dry run session. Make sure the team is aligned.

2. Give your reps time to fail at this. This may be a big transformational shift for your team and it may not go well the first couple of times. But my experience is

that if you are prepared with the right intent, it usually turns out just right.

3. If you go, understand your role from the rep. Don't dictate your role. Make sure the rep is clear about the relationships you are responsible for in the meeting breaks.

4. I've seen a number of sales managers show up wanting their reps to present and sell. Buy into the process and just like a baseball manager, only step in as it relates to your role in winning the game. Don't go into the field to catch a fly ball. You are there to help, but not take the mic and own the stage. You will burn trust forever if you do this.

5. Do a wrap session with the team that was a part of the joint-envisioning. Reflect and learn. You will have a team of reps doing this slightly differently based on their style. Try to take "lessons learned" and incorporate them into a weekly sales meeting.

Chapter 11

Proposals Shmo-posals

A few years ago, I was introduced to a new slick software application that was supposed to help streamline and bring consistency to proposals our company was submitting. The software walked the rep through a set of questions about the specific products and services being offered to the client. It also gave the opportunity to edit and customize specifically to the client. When you were finished creating the proposal, you entered the client's email address and "poof" it was emailed to them. As part of the process, the software could tell you when they opened it, forwarded it, and if they "accepted it." I am in no way trying to bash the efforts of this application, but in my experience this was as commoditizing as it comes. Every rep I interviewed told me that 90% of the time the client just went to the pricing detail when they received the email linking back to the proposal.

Think about when you are on the car lot looking to purchase a new car. You look at the cars and find the style and color you like the most. Then you walk to the window sticker and look at the pricing details. It's how we, as buyers, are conditioned to behave. So, sending the proposal out in this way leads the buyer to avoid reading the pages of marketing *gobblygook* found in most proposals and go straight to the pricing. Unless you are the cheapest product on the market and are trying to commoditize your competition, this approach hurts you in your process. Why? Because you are commoditizing yourself just like we talked about in Chapter 4. Why would you want use the correct sales process all the way up to proposal and then commoditize yourself in the process by sending a document? It makes no sense to me and this is why we don't recommend this process to our clients.

I find that a lot of hardware or parts sales people are so used to getting an order for a specific part that they often just send quotes. There is a place for this type of selling practice. I find in the complex sales process consisting of more than two conversations, sending a quote/paper proposal does not work consistently. There is always a sales manager or a sales rep who wants to tell me the story of how it works. At JumpSetter, we are not just trying to help our clients win a deal. We are trying to help you help your client be successful in their project. So, let's explore what that looks like.

Back in my early days of doing this work, I was working with Rick, a VP of Sales who wanted leadership, sales training, and coaching for his entire team, including himself. We met and went through the entire sales process, as I have described to you in this book. Rick and JumpSetter were on the same page and it was clear there was a strategic and cultural fit between our two organizations. Rick had also kept the president of the company updated on the progress of the project. As it got close to the time where we were going to finalize the opportunity and move to the contract phase, the president started asking a lot of questions Rick wasn't prepared to answer. Rick was frustrated. He had a paper proposal from us that he sent to the president and had talked with him about what he wanted to accomplish. Rick came back, frustrated and embarrassed, it was at that moment I realized I had done him no favors in my approach. Even though I had walked him through the proposal, the president didn't read the text document in detail. He read the pricing detail and began asking questions similar to what your dad would ask when you wanted $25 for Friday evening.

From that point on, I have never sent just a paper proposal (no matter how good) to a client. On paper, I can't show them how we can help. Canned proposals, quotes or PowerPoint presentations, do not consistently and sufficiently help our clients.

From my experience, the person, "the champion" you are working with on the buyer's side, may have to do his own presentation for approval or may ask you to do a presentation on their behalf to gain approval from his board or executive committee. Depending on what you are selling and the culture of the organization, this may even be to the president of the corporation. We have to build a presentation that enables the champion to run with the information required for him to gain approval. I literally tell my prospects that I will be building my proposal in a presentation format that they will be able to run with and communicate the *"Why JumpSetter"* message. They will be presenting *"Why JumpSetter"* and *"Why Now"* to whomever is approving the project. Sending a paper proposal they didn't read only to have them send it to someone else who didn't read it, isn't helping them or you. For you to be successful, you need to help your champion be successful with the project you have both invested so much time in.

For the benefit of helping you remember the process we are getting ready to teach, I want you to remember **RSAPA**. That is the acronym that will enable you to remember the process. Let's walk through **RSAPA** and help you begin implementing it today.

Recap

You have held multiple meetings with different people, gathering information about goals, challenges, concerns, and success criteria. This is your opportunity to put this into a format that will allow you to show the potential buyer you listened and weren't just giving them superficial attention. Because of what buyers and companies have experienced or the stories they have heard, there is a perspective out there that reps just want to sell and hit quota. You have used the process in this book to help differentiate yourself from those reps, now prove it, by recapping what you heard and tying it all together in one or two slides. They meet with so many companies, they may not remember what they previously told you. This is your chance to validate, add, or change. You must do this so it is clear you are on the same page with them. But it should also allow them to articulate upstream in the approval process exactly what the goals, success criteria, and concerns/risks are in the project. I've had a few clients say they don't want to share those concerns in the proposal. Have the conversation and listen to their concerns. They probably know the culture and have experienced or seen this process work in their organization before. I personally try to include those concerns and list them as risks in the project. You will have the opportunity to clear up how you are going to address them in the next two sections of this document.

Solution

This is your chance to list the specific solution you are putting in place with them. This is not where you go crazy, telling them all the cool features about your product and services. This is your opportunity to recap why this solution is exactly what you landed on in the joint-envisioning session. There should be no surprises from where you landed in that last meeting. How does this solution help them accomplish their goals, enable their success criteria, and overcome the risks/concerns they shared? This is where the doctor tells you about the surgery he is going to perform, how he's going to prepare your knee for the operation, and what he'll do that is going to allow you to return to your indoor soccer league. He will explain why it's the right surgery for this particular injury. The conversation is so you can understand why this surgery mitigates the risks he already shared with you, but also addresses the concerns he shared with you. Be more of a doctor in this approach and less of the "slick willy sales guy."

Don't overdo the number of slides either, by including all the canned marketing slides your organization typically wants you to present. Customize these slides to explicitly state why this solution is going to help them with the information you recapped in the "R" section of this presentation. Keep it simple and make sure it's information that will help bring clarity. If you find yourself adding something in an attempt to persuade or convince: stop. Readjust your thinking and focus on the intent to enrich your champion to be successful.

Approach

You have recapped and shared your solution. This is your opportunity to share the approach your organization is going to take to ensure this is a successful project. This is different than the "solution" in that the solution is about the specific products and services. This is more the approach you are taking to the overall project to assure longterm success and not just get them up and running. In the solution section, I described how the surgeon explains why the specific knee surgery is perfect for you. This is where he describes the approach to make sure the knee surgery not only works, but is successful post-surgery. From a technology sales standpoint, this is where you explain your implementation process, ongoing support process, and overall approach to ongoing service, as it relates to enabling their goals, success criteria, and overcoming their concerns. This is not a time for you to explain why you are better than your competition. Don't make this about you. It is a time for you to show them a clear view of how this approach is going to enable success as they have defined it.

Pricing

This is your opportunity to present the pricing to the client that is tied to the solution and the approach you just described to them. I've seen many approaches to this section. How you present your pricing is dependent on the type of product and service you are selling. This is something we work on with our clients individually, so we can help them present it in the best format to fit their industry. My rule of thumb is to list out the specific products and services they are getting and then show a total monthly fee, one time fees, and basic terms. I may sometimes show the discounting too, so they see and feel they are getting a "deal." Most people want to think they got a deal. I do not include any optional products and services on this slide. If you believe you should be doing it, include it. If it's optional from your perspective, it is probably optional in their perspective and you are telling them you don't believe it is necessary for success. You have shared the solution to meet their goals, success criteria, and concerns. If something isn't needed to do this, why would you be proposing it?

I believe itemized pricing works towards a menu approach to selling. Unless it's something you have to absolutely do, I recommend not doing it. It doesn't matter what they want to see, it's a matter of how you present it. You can't help them if they are going to try to compare your pieces and parts line by line and itemize you to death. I love to ask them questions like:

- How is itemized pricing going to help you make your decision or gain approval on this project? If it isn't going to, have your answer planned to rebut this.

They may answer by saying they are trying to review options. This is why I try to avoid pricing options, but rather price the solution that you jointly came to in the joint-envisioning session. Options are price-based, solutions are need-based. This section could be a chapter in itself and I'm not going to break it all down for you, but this should give you the concept of the P in RSAPA.

Assumptions

I remember back in 2003, I was working with a company in Nebraska on a project. After an underling called me for pricing and product info, I was able to get to the president fairly quickly. It's one of those cases where she and her president were on a call with me about two hours after our intro call. At the end of the call, he said, "Let's go."

I had the contracts drawn up and he signed them the next day. What was normally a 90-120 day sales cycle was over in less than seventy-two hours. Some may call it a bluebird deal (meaning it came easy), but I call it a disaster. Sure I got paid, and sure we eventually got it implemented successfully, but every time someone tells me they want to move fast, I cringe. The client and I were not as aligned as we both thought we were. An "assumptions" slide is your opportunity to align expectations with the client. Who is responsible for what? When would payments be due? How long this pricing is offered and the ramifications of missing the pricing offer? There are infinite assumptions depending upon the opportunity and your organization. Setting proper expectation is the purpose of assumptions. It validates that you are not guessing and it protects you from the client mouthing "the rep told me this."

Now that you have your five-ten slide RSAPA Project Overview, set up a time to walk through, and verify the information with the client. Similar to the joint-envisioning meeting, try to get the decision-makers in the meeting when you walk through it. I typically send an Adobe document a few hours before we are scheduled to walk through the presentation. The key word is "scheduled." I don't send it, if we are not scheduled, as doing so may eliminate me immediately. Don't present it, talk through it. It should be an executive summary of everything you have already discussed and jointly decided except for the pricing and assumptions. When all of your competitors send their documents, you will indeed give them another experience that will separate you from those who get "commoditized" by their own process. Beyond that, your champion has a very clear presentation document that he can walk through with others in his organization to get the buy-in needed to be successful. It's a simple and beautiful thing they should find valuable.

Old Thinking said: The client wants pricing and I'm going to send them a proposal.

New Thinking says: I am going to help my client understand the value of what we jointly agreed to in a simple, easy document, that I walk them through.

Reflection for the Sales Representative

1. No matter where you are in any deal, change your process on this now. If you have a proposal due tomorrow; change your approach. If you set an expectation differently than what you just read, call the client in the morning and tell him that something inside you felt like it was better for them to go this route to help your client be successful. What's the worst thing that could happen?

2. If you don't know the answers to the sections above, you are missing steps in your sales process. Figure it out! You are robbing your client of the best chance to be successful with you.

Reflection for the Sales Manager

1. Forget what marketing wants you to send, this is about helping the client and rep work successfully together for the best chance to succeed. If your company requires the paper document, then have them send it with the RSAPA document after the walk through meeting. Just make sure that nothing conflicts between the two documents.

2. This RSAPA process should help you realize if your rep understands as much about this project as he or she thinks they do. Don't test them, help walk through what is being proposed and help them map it back to the goals, success criteria, and risks. Don't tell them what to do, help them learn by asking great questions that don't lead them to the answer you want. Leading the witness isn't creating an environment of learning.

CHAPTER 12

SHE SAID YES!
NOW WHAT?

The time has finally come! You got the verbal affirmation from the client that you are their solution of choice and they want to move forward with you and your organization. The emotions from hearing those words are so rewarding. It's like getting the note back from the girl in third grade that has the word "yes" circled. You know, the note that was passed to her that says, "I like you, do you like me? Circle one: yes or no or maybe so."

And she just passed it back "yes." That was my modus operandi when I was school...

College coaches recruit high school student-athletes to play for their schools. Before signing the letter of intent with the university (which is a contract), athletes may hold a press conference or make a simple call to the coach, verbally telling the coach of their intentions. The act of giving the verbal commitment to a coach is not binding in any way, but it is a way of showing intent. I call the act of a client giving a verbal commitment to move forward with us, "verballing." So, you have received the verbal confirmation. She said YES! Now what?

I remember a time when I had a client in Arizona who had "verballed" to me and said the contract was coming via fax that same day. He told me he just got the contract signed and was heading to the fax machine to send the contract for us to counter sign. I waited and waited, but it didn't show up. Four days later, he explained that on his way to the fax machine, the president of the organization stopped him because their organization had just reached agreement to be purchased. Like this example, there are many reasons why after a verbal deal stalls or maybe never happens. Bill Busch, who is one of the best reps I know, always said, "Nothing good happens between yes and signing a contract."

Unless you are new to sales, you have experienced this thing we call "slippage" in the industry. They slip past the expected close dates like a car sliding past the expected stop sign at an icy intersection. Just like that car, bad things usually happen when deals slip past the initial timeline. Slippage might be the most frustrating thing in any sales organization. Slippage creates so many issues. Reps thought it was a "done deal," and sales management counted on it, setting up pipeline projections clear up to the board and investors. Now management is coming at you like an angry driver you just t-boned in the intersection, to get details as to why this deal is slipping past the mark. You may have heard the phrase *time kills deals*, and to a degree it is correct because it's only a matter of time before something that comes up shifting priorities. Like my story above about the acquisition, it stops the whole process altogether after you've invested months into the project.

Here are some of the management responses reps have reported that came from slippage:

- Yelled at to get in there and "close" that deal.
- Are you even asking the right questions or are you just flat out guessing?
- Calling out the rep for committing this project and not delivering the project as expected!

- The BOSS is taking over, because you clearly can't do this on your own.
- Micromanaging the rep and dictating exactly how to get this baby closed.
- Go sit in the lobby of their company and wait until your guy walks through and ask him what the heck is going on with this?

I laugh out loud thinking about how people behave and the culture they create with these types of responses. As ludicrous as these responses sound and the culture that the behavior fosters, the truth is as reps, we are as guilty as anyone for letting this happen. Many times we heard the "yes" and stopped being skeptical and asking great questions. Look, I will be the first to say that you can't make anyone do anything they don't want to. If you do silver-tongue talk them into doing it, they may never trust you again, if it isn't the most amazing experience. The whole approach of this book is not to "push/pull" the client over the finish line to the contract signing. The above responses spit in the face of everything you have been trying to build and show in your sales culture. You don't want that and your sales managers don't want that either. In addition, it destroys relationships and trust. If you don't think so, go to a timeshare meeting on your next vacation and "enjoy" that process. Sit there in a conference room for two hours as you are passed through layers of sales management, three to five times, because you won't say "yes." It especially stinks when you could have spent that time lying by the pool with your favorite drink.

So let's not let this happen to us. Let's work with our clients jointly to avoid this thing called "slippage." It's not that hard! Let me explain how to get a buy-in from your client around their milestones and deadlines. And we need to get them to see it as affirmation you are right. We call this a

Mutual Action Plan or MAP. This is a rep's "project" plan you and the client work on together and jointly partner in building the steps of a plan that will bring about an engagement of the two organizations.

I was working with a client in St. Louis and they just gave me the verbal that they wanted to move forward with us on a $6.5 million project. As we discussed their reasons for picking my company and began to shift to next steps, I told them about MAP. I shared with them the value my clients had received working with me through the process. I showed the client an example of a MAP and explained how the process worked. I then asked if she would be open to setting up a meeting to work through it?

I still remember how she told me, "Brandon, you just validated everything you told me you would do from the beginning. Your willingness to help us is so wonderfully appreciated."

Imagine that, I got to set proper expectations around all the rest of the steps and they love me for it? What's that tell you?

People just want you to help them be successful. Remember, most people have the voice in the back of their head telling them they are not smart enough, can't do this, are making a bad decision, run! Your willingness to show them a path to success continues to show the experience you promised with your "personal value statement" at your introduction, and you didn't change when "She said yes!"

Here is how the process works:

1. Before you hold your MAP meeting, proactively list the phases and steps for each phase you feel need to be completed by both your organization and theirs.
2. Now put them in logical order based on the order you think you are going to need to accomplish them. For

example, you can't get a signature on the contract before legal reviews docs and your legal can't review the redlines, if they have not redlined them yet. So think through this process based on your experiences.

3. Now ask yourself, *what has caused slippage before* and get proactive with this. Don't short cut the list. How can the signer sign the contract on the last day of the quarter, if she is on vacation in Fiji the last two weeks of the quarter? Add those things in there.

4. Beside every item, assign an owner and a target completion date while also marking hard dates that can't be missed (aka board meeting date.)

5. Meet with the client and work through the process together. Get them to add or delete things based on how their process works. You will find out rather quickly if they know how the process works in their organization. If they don't know, how are you going to figure it out?

6. Who is on vacation or out of office during remaining phases of the MAP that would put the project timeline at risk.

You get the gist of where we are going with this. I am not going to put it all in this chapter, but this will have you headed in the right direction. Here is the bottom line: if you don't get them to take joint ownership of this document with you, you run the risk of slippage.

I remember I was working with Debby, who, by the way, is one of my favorite clients of all time. She was such a sponge, eager to get better and learn so she could help her clients. She loved working with her clients and her intent was so pure that her clients fell in love with her. Debby had just finalized a contract with a client who had gone six months past the expected close time. The pressure her organization put on her in that time was nearly unbearable, but she got it closed. She came to me and said, "Help me to never feel this, ever again."

I taught her about the Mutual Action Plan. She went out on faith on her next project when she received verbal and got the client to buy into the process. They jointly built a plan and assigned dates and ownership. The next day, the client emailed her, asking her to add these additional steps and modify the dates. Now, do you think this helped Debby set better expectations internally around this project? Do you think it helped the champion on the client side to set correct expectations with his internal organization? Debby closed this fourteen-month sales process worth more than $3 million in quota credit two days after the project was originally projected.

Another time, I was working with a major foundation out of New York City. After receiving the verbal, I worked with the CIO on a MAP. The project closed one day earlier than expected because we virtually eliminated any risk of slippage. You can't eliminate everything, but you can work towards it!

Be flexible because not everything is going to go the way you laid it out at the beginning. Nothing ever goes that easily! It's about recalibrating together and updating expectations internally. This process has worked extreamly well. It's why we built the MAP consulting plan to work directly with companies that want to enable reps to mutually manage details easily and effectively align with their clients.

Don't complicate the process. I have seen reps and managers jump into the idea of *let's get the client to buy into a MAP* at the first meeting and lay out the whole sales process in that initial conversation. Okay, while there might be some logic here, our experience tells us that it is better received after the client has emotionally bought into you and your organization. Remember, 90% of all reps are attention deficit and are not project managers. You can barely get them to enter notes in CRM, so don't complicate this into being more than what its purpose is. Help the client and rep have one common set of expectations that will work towards finalizing the partnership in a signed agreement.

Old Thinking: I got the verbal, and I need to understand their process so I can work towards closing this process.

New Thinking: When I get verbal, I help my client think through the process with me to make sure there no surprises or missed steps that would throw their project off timeline.

Reflection for the Sales Representative

1. Make a list of all the examples of a time when you had slippage and why?
2. Is the process different for your different product lines?
3. If you skip this step in the process, you are missing an amazing opportunity to affirm the decision to do business with you. You will be surprised at how much this step will strengthen your relationship with your client.
4. If you are not making the move to this approach immediately, what is holding you back and how is it going to eliminate the risk of slippage?

Reflection for the Sales Manager

1. For the love of all leadership books ever written, please don't panic and treat your reps horribly when slippage happens. Hold them accountable appropriately and help them learn. Ask good questions and watch them grow. Tear them down and you will lose them. I've seen it too many times and it ends up that I get the privilege of training and coaching them at their new provider. What is the culture you are trying to build? What is your purpose as a sales leader?

2. Think about how you can use the MAP to set expectations to the rest of the organization around pipeline forecasts. How can you use these to eliminate questions that don't help bring the project to finalization?

3. How can you help remove obstacles internally to help your own organization hit the timelines as laid out in the MAP?

Chapter 13

Ignoring Red Lights Kills

Over the years, I've identified several God-given traits of great sales people. We can teach, we can help people grow, and we can help people get out of their own way mentally, but we can't impart God-given talent. Two of the most important traits are:

1. The ability to hold a conversation. If you can't hold a conversation on the fly without a script, then maybe a sales career isn't right for you.
2. The ability to recognize the yellow or red light warning signs in real time. When something doesn't sound right or doesn't add up in a conversation, does this person catch on? If you can't detect those little red flags, please pick a different career as you are going to significantly struggle.

For the purposes of this chapter, we are going to focus on the second trait and talk about the importance of leveraging that skill so you can help your clients and separate yourself from the competition. What happens when you just blow through a red light? Sometimes nothing. Usually this is because you got lucky. However, the majority of the time, the obvious answer is you get into an accident, you have a run in with the police, or in the worst case scenario, you die. Having the ability to recognize warning signs is critical to knowing whether or not you need to slow down or stop to avoid an impending disaster. Ignoring warning signs in a sales conversation works exactly the same way.

Some reps can see the warning flag in the middle of the sales conversation, but for some reason they feel that ignoring it will make it go away or the situation to work itself out. In actuality, the opposite is more than likely to happen. Have you ever driven at night in the fog? You can sometimes see the road, road signs, and potential obstacles, and other times it's a "white knuckled" experience as you grip the steering wheel for dear life, hoping and praying you don't crash. Pretty much every single one of us would prefer driving at night with full clarity and without fog, but that's not always the situation we find ourselves in. Sometimes you have to stop or even slow down until you have clarity. And sometimes you have no choice but to get through the thick of it. In the same way, for some reason, sales reps believe ambiguity is okay when it's actually like a fog that we are trying to navigate through during the sales process. Pretending it doesn't exist only sets you up to crash because of what you can't see. But if you would have just paused until you had clarity, you could have seen exactly how to maneuver appropriately.

There was a time when I was working with a rep named Dave and he was nervous about having a difficult conversation with a client. Dave feared it would cause the client to dislike him and decide not to do business with him. Dave said his prospect told him the president of the company was not going to be involved in this project or the decision-making process. She claimed the president trusted her to do all the research and make the decision. I asked Dave, "In your industry, based on the importance of this product to the business, have you ever seen this be the case?" Dave said he had never had a case where the president of a company would allow this to happen, but this lady was confident, adamant, and aggressive. And this was a big project, important to the company. To set the stage, this would be the equivalent of a man telling a realtor his wife didn't need to see the house before he made an offer on it. Now, I don't know about you, but my wife would never let me spend hundreds of thousands of dollars on a home, where she would have to live, decorate, and manage our lives, without seeing it firsthand. Dave's situation was no different, but his fear of losing, based upon offending her or causing her to become aggressive, was causing him to blow through the red light warning sign.

While there is some truth to the idea that saving a difficult conversation for a one-on-one situation and not in front of a whole group has logic, that wasn't the case here. Many times, the fear of losing holds us back. Other times it is our inability to detach (as we discussed earlier in the book) that keeps us from having the conversations that need to happen. But in this particular situation, the good news was that Dave, at least, saw the warning signs. He may have been seeking to avoid the flashing red light at the railroad crossing, but he recognized something was amiss. If he wasn't seeing the red light or failed to see it, maybe Dave might want to reevaluate the direction of his career. Sometimes, the best way to learn about red lights and warning signs is to experience them or to learn from observing others' situations.

While this chapter is not going to dive into the details there are many books on handling difficult conversations.

Instead, let's discuss a couple of the most common "Red Lights." We have already discussed not having the correct decision-makers involved in the process, so that is an important situation to be aware of.

RED LIGHT: The company has no intent to change but just wants to get a better offer from its current provider.

So many organizations use their vendor process to review "options" during the contract renewal year so they can negotiate a better deal with their current provider. I've seen companies hire consultants, go through a full RFP process, sit through hours of demos, and even go on client visits, all so they can renew with their current provider at a lower price.

If you miss the warning signs for this type of situation, you will be dragged through a whole sales process and a waste of time. You will be left looking like you got played... *because you did.* Nothing is more frustrating than to invest months, resources, and cash into a project only to learn the client did nothing but stay right where they were.

Have you heard any of these comments before?

"Our current contract with Vendor A is a few months away from auto renewal and we wanted to see what other options are out there."

"Our current provider nickel and dimes us to death and we are tired of it."

"We just are not happy with the service of our current provider and want to explore options."

All of those statements exist in deals you may win or lose. I am not saying that every time you hear these types of comments the buyer is falsely representing his intentions. I am simply stating that when you hear things like this, you have to stay on topic and dive in to figure out if they have driving force to change. So often, we take these words at face value and move forward, blindly trusting.

In contrast, this is where I have watched reps move forward because they think they can convince the buyer to change. My experience is you can't convince anyone to do anything they really don't want to do; especially when other logical thinkers are going to have to justify and approve the change. Depending on what your market is and what you sell, sometimes the move from one platform to another can feel like "heart surgery" for the organization. Even if you have a history of heart disease in your family, you don't go in for heart surgery unless you need to. This is because the interruption it will bring to your life, the recovery period, the change in personality, and the expense is not worth it unless you absolutely need to. It's when your strategy to live is impeded that you are willing to go through the surgery to make sure you stay alive. In many cases, this same situation is happening with the deal you are trying to close; there is either a driving force with a compelling event or there isn't. Get out of the game of "convincing" and focus on understanding "the driving force for change" as well as "the compelling event," or you will quite possibly get killed by the red light you ignored early on.

RED LIGHT: The game has changed and you don't see it.

In a Big Ten college championship football game, I watched Penn State and Wisconsin play. In the first quarter Wisconsin owned the line of scrimmage on both sides of the ball. Their defense was stuffing the run and putting pressure on the Penn State quarterback. On offense, Wisconsin was putting together nine-minute, fifteen-play drives. It looked as if it was Wisconsin's game to win. Penn State evaluated the situation at haltime and had to make in-game adjustments. The changes they deployed began to change the game. They fought back to win the game by seven. As my friends and I watched the game, we commented about how the game completely changed in the second half. In many complex sales situations, you have a number of conversations with the client. Through that process of evaluating the information the client has provided and working to help them, you sometimes hear the client say something that is much different than what you heard before. Just like the football game, the sales situation requires a change in the game-plan. At least you recognized the fact that the client said something different than what you heard before, which can be either perceived by you as positive or negative. Either way, ignoring the change is ignoring a red light. Ambiguity around a perceived positive or negative doesn't usually serve you well.

Let's look at an example of this and the importance of not ignoring the warning of the game-changing moment.

One of my reps was working with an organization for a number of months on a complex technology project. The rep told me that the organization was intrigued and contemplating us and his main competitor. The potential client had been reserved in sharing much about the differences between our approaches and the competition's proposed differences. After an onsite meeting, as our rep was shaking hands to leave, the CIO said he believed we were the right company, based on the meeting they just had, and he wanted to get this project wrapped up contractually. Yes, any rep would like hearing this, but the change by itself was a red light the rep ignored and took at face value. Two weeks later, our rep was informed the client had chosen our competitor. Hearing what you want to hear can be bad, if you don't remain inquisitive and dive-in to learn how the client came to a conclusion, good or bad. If the rep would have just said something like, "I'd like to setup some time with you to understand your thoughts around us and this project," he would have probably learned how real the comment was or what the weakness in the logic was. Instead, he ignored the red light and the deal died.

Sometimes the game-changing moments are subtler than the last example I shared. The lesson here is to pay attention and have the conversation to get a better understanding. Both positive and negatively perceived changes can be disastrous, if you ignore them and don't dive into understanding the validity of the change. When the game changes and you don't understand and adjust, you increase the odds of not being able to help and ultimately losing.

There are a number of many other red lights you will encounter. Learn from them, and avoid running into them in the future. Stay calm in both situations whether the direction of the sale is perceived negatively or positively. You are the leader of this opportunity. Keep your team calm as well. Seek the truth, tell good stories, and ask great questions. "The short way is usually the long way and the long way is the short way." This is so true, as it relates to these red lights. If you short cut the way by ignoring them, it can create a long and painful path. Ambiguity is not your friend, clarity is.

Old Thinking: *"I'll ignore that and hope it goes away, while moving forward in the project."*

New Thinking: *"I can't ignore warning signs as they more than often will cause me problems later."*

Reflection for the Sales Representative:

1. Think back to deals you thought were going your way and then you lost. What were the red lights you missed causing the deal to crash?
2. What points did you have before then to actually have the conversation you needed to have? Remember, our job is to get the truth and ask good questions and share stories, not make their decisions for them.

Reflection for the Sales Manager:

1. When was a situation where one of your reps came to you with new information about a project that took you by surprise as compared to what you expected from previous conversations? What could you have done differently to help coach your rep instead of trying to fix the deal?
2. When you are doing deal-review or you are in the client meeting and you hear or see red lights do you feel free to ask questions to seek clarity? Think back to when you did and when you didn't feel it was appropriate, what were the differences in those situations?

CHAPTER 14

BE A LEADER

There are a ton of books on leadership. As you know from previous chapters, I am a huge follower of John Maxwell's leadership philosophies. Stephen Covey is another great source of leadership teachings that can impact your life tremendously.

I was sitting on a call with John Maxwell when he said, "Everything rises and falls with leadership." When he said those words, I interpreted them as, "It's all in how you lead that determines the fate of your organization." In other words, you are where you are, because you led yourself to this point. You are either going to rise or you are going to fall depending upon the leadership you demonstrate. He didn't say everything rises and falls with "management." He didn't say everything rises and falls on "hope" or "strategy." He didn't say everything rises and falls on your smartest people. But rather everything rises and falls on "leadership."

Most sales people don't manage people. As I stated earlier, in many organizations we confuse management with leadership. Leadership is about your ability to influence others. Over the years, I have learned that there are many opportunities to lead. As sales reps, you:

1. Lead your clients
2. Lead your team
3. Lead your families

Let's take a look at each of these and make sure you are being the leader others will follow to success:

1. Lead Your Clients

As we have discussed already in this book, the most obvious place you have to lead is with your clients. You have the ability to help them and invest in them so they have the ability to have success. Go back to the definition of success defined in Chapter One. Stay true to that definition as you focus on no longer being the persuader, but being a person of connection and influence for your client's success.

2. Lead Your Team

Many people in sales careers have an engagement team who has worked with them in order to accomplish the goals of specific meetings in sales situations and processes. Those may be sales engineers, consultants, and advisors, but those can also be executive and sales management you are pulling into a meeting. You count on them just like a quarterback on the football team counts on each of his teammates to move the ball down the field. Yet for some reason, too often, reps fail to take the leadership steps necessary to move the sales opportunity down the field with their teammates. This idea of letting your engagement team show up and do their "thing" without you leading and organizing them is a recipe for failure. No matter who you are pulling in, they want to be successful for you, successful for the client, and successful for themselves. If you don't set them up to succeed, these teammates can crash the meeting and the entire team fails. Lead and organize your team with clear expectations and messaging!

You might be asking, "Brandon, are you telling me that I am to lead my boss or even his boss in my meetings?" Yes, that is exactly the expectation I am setting in your mind. You are the leader of your territory and your opportunities. Each member of your team is a club in your golf bag that you have to use to have success based on the situation. If you let the driver in your bag take control on the green, you not only will miss your putts but you will more than likely get kicked off the course. It is important to lead all of the teammates you pull into your opportunities. Here are some steps I recommend to help with your ability to lead your team.

a) *It Starts With a Relationship* – If you don't have a personal relationship with your team and you are expected to lead them, you are putting yourself and your team at risk. Your ability to lead comes from your ability to connect and influence. Those things come from getting to know each member. I use every opportunity to get to know my teammates and understand who they are, how they got here, and where they are going. I want to understand what success looks like to them in their personal growth. My goal is to work with them to make sure I just don't accomplish my goals, but as much, if not more importantly, what success looks like to them and how they accomplish their goals. A great leader knows the members of his team and has a connection with them.

b) *Establish Your Team's Culture* – If you are not all aligned on the philosophy as to what your definition of success is for this project, this meeting, or this conversation, and one person shows up "selling and pitching," then you are not aligned in culture. The team won't perform in the way that validates the expectations you set with the client and success will begin to tilt toward failure. Share your story of what your intent is and why. Let them connect to your story and gain buy-in. Ask questions to validate their understanding and comfort. If someone is not buying-in immediately, then maybe you don't include them in this meeting, but don't give up. Change does not happen overnight. More often than not, people will follow your lead around this situation. If someone falls back into old habits, be patient with them and wait until after the meeting to reflect. Leaders define the culture.

c) *Be Clear With Expectations and Agenda* – Spend time aligning what *they* expect to bring to the meeting with what *you* expect from them. All too often, the assumption of expectation is what creates the biggest conflict or point of failure. The quarterback and his wide receivers have to be on the same page on what route to run, when to run it, and when to expect the ball to be there. Leaders don't fly by the seat of their pants. Don't be a control freak. Be open to ideas and concepts that fit the direction you are navigating the team. One person's ability to point out the iceberg may have saved the Titanic. Leaders navigate the team while listening and aligning expectations.

d) *Have the Team Prepared* – How good would a team be if they only read their playbook and didn't practice the plays before the big game? Rarely do teams like practice. Some people often create excuses about how practice makes them tired or doesn't keep them mentally fresh. Those are nothing short of world-class excuses. To be prepared for the success of your client, you owe it to that client to be prepared and to have your team prepared. Yes, your presentation is created. Yes, you have discussed expectations. Now just like the day before the opening of the premier of a play, do a dry run where you walk through the agenda and recap the goals which were already shared with the team. Review the presentation, having each person discuss the key points they will cover and why. Talk through possible challenges you expect to encounter and discuss with the team how you want to handle those situations. One hour of prep the night before a four-hour meeting the next day will, more often than not, have the team confident and prepared to help your client. Leaders have their team prepared.

e) *Orchestrate the Meeting* – A year ago, I had the privilege to be five feet away from the Orlando Philharmonic Orchestra as they were directed by "a leadership consultant," the conductor. The job of the conductor is to guide each musician and each section of instruments through the song, providing perfection to the ear of the audience. I've seen too many reps allow a meeting to get away from them because they were not keeping the team aligned and in sync. When you see the meeting getting off topic and getting away from you, be the leader who calls time out and pulls the team and client back together for the success of the goals established. Of course, there are times that an unplanned conversation may need to take place, but more often than not, everyone will appreciate the tabling of that as a "to-do" coming from the meeting rather than derailing the whole meeting. I've seen reps let senior management or sales management take their meeting off track, only to watch it crash. Do not let anyone fail the client, no matter what their role is on the team. Leaders facilitate the meeting while orchestrating the team.

f) *Leaders Reflect* – Without reflection, more often than not, experience is lost and wasted. Set up a time to reflect with your team for a time of learning. John Maxwell says the best teacher in life is not experience, but reflected experience. Give your team a chance to reflect and learn and discuss how they would do it differently next time, where to go next, and the steps to get there. Leaders enable growth through reflection without condemnation.

3. Lead Your Family

You run. You work. You travel. You communicate. All of these things you do frequently and you do them hard. You do this because you are a professional, working towards helping your clients and serving our co-workers, all for the success of both organizations. There is something rewarding about hard work and a clean conscience, knowing you are doing your best professionally (at least that's what the best of the best do). Some of you may be still trying to shortcut your way there. As much I have found myself at times working at all hours of the day for weeks and months, if we fail to lead those to whom we are most responsible, we get out of balance. Great leaders have balance.

I don't know about you, but as much as I enjoy helping sales professionals reach new heights in their life professional and financially, I do all of it for the success of my family. We, as reps, in our pursuit of success cannot forget who we are here to honor and lead. Our coaches work with our clients through John Maxwell's *Wheel of Life*. The whole goal of the system is to figure out regularly if the people we are working with have clarity about where they are in different facets of their life; do they have balance? Without balance, things begin to tilt and that is when you fall. I've worked with reps over the years who have seen their pursuit of financial gain, lead them to forgo the responsibilities to their family and ultimately lose it. I am not saying you shouldn't do what is necessary, but the "for every force there is an equal and opposite force" thinking comes into play. If you have to sacrifice and travel three weeks in a row for your profession, find the equal but opposite force to balance that out after the fact. Invest in your partner. Invest in your kids. At the end of the day, that is what life is all about. Helping your family find that balance will enable you to reduce those pressures that may hold you back from doing what you feel you need to do professionally. Follow the steps in this chapter and use the same philosophy with your family (to some degree). Invest in the relationships. Discuss your family goals and the set expectations around your professional career to accomplish those goals. Communicate your schedule and opportunities with your family. Plan your time with them intentionally to grow. Reflect on the balance of family and work and make decisions on where to go from that point forward.

Old Thinking: "*We are all professionals, we don't need practice or preparation.*"

New Thinking: "*Because we are professionals, we will be prepared to help our client.*"

Reflection for the Sales Representative:

1. Who on your team do you have relationships with versus those you don't? How can you invest in all of them?
2. Define your culture/beliefs, expectations and be prepared to communicate that. When should you do that before the meeting? Who do you need to include?
3. Set expectation of travel or availability to do dry runs and discuss expectations. When the team wants to go, get dinner, relax, and forgo this step, how will you be prepared to handle this?

4. How can you facilitate reflection with the team and document the learnings and new opportunities for growth?

Reflection for the Sales Manager:

1. How can you set your reps up to follow this without dictating it? How can you help your team see the importance of this and not make it feel like an unnecessary task?

2. How can you make sure you don't take over a meeting, allowing your rep to lead? It is important to be vulnerable, allowing your rep to learn and grow through her experiences. Typically, assuring preparedness will help you let the team go. Teaching is done through practice, not during the game. We have all heard that parent-coach yelling from the sideline during the game, trying to teach. In the game, it's too late. Let them go and learn from there in the time of reflection.

3. How can you help your rep without condemnation? Condemnation tears down relationship and trust.

CHAPTER 15

DON'T GO ALONE

When I was growing up, Bruce Lee movies were a big hit. The guy could not just leverage martial arts, he was known for his tremendous speed kicks and punches that would leave the average person standing in awe. I could envision myself being this karate warrior who could take on the strongest of all foes with my cat-like martial arts skills. Unfortunately, we didn't have the money for lessons. There also wasn't a maintenance man named Mr. Miagi in our neighborhood who took me under his wing to teach me. At our elementary school library, I found a book on karate. I went home and studied that book. I would be in my room kicking and punching stacked pillows. In the movie, *The Karate Kid*, Daniel (the boy who is being bullied at the new school), is doing this exact same thing when Mr. Miagi comes to his apartment to do some maintenance work. He looks at Daniel and asks, "You are learning karate from a book?"

That scene called into question the ability to master something from a book. Just like I tried, Daniel trained himself hard by the book, but he continued to get dominated by the bullies who were karate black belts. If you have seen the movie, you know how absurd it was to think you could master karate from a book and be good enough to compete against those who were being trained by a master. It was when Daniel began to work with Mr. Miagi, a seasoned master, that he gained the mental strength and skill to begin the process of actually being able to defend himself.

There was a time in history when Tiger Woods was mopping up on the golf course. He was dominating every event in which he was competing. I remember watching him in his first Masters not only compete, but win by the largest stroke lead ever. It seemed like he was at a whole new level. In an interview, he talked about how he had worked the previous week with his coach on his short game. It paid off because he was sinking his putts. Previously, putting was probably the only weakness in his game. I remember thinking, "Tiger has a coach?" The guy is the best golfer in the world and yet he still has a coach? I just couldn't understand why a guy who was playing better than any golfer in history would need a coach.

I meet sales managers and sales reps all the time and I ask them if they are working with a coach. The answer 99.99% of the time is "no," as if it's a good thing to say "no." They talk about reading books, which is great, but as we have learned, it's very hard to take a book and turn what is read into a mastered skill. Can you imagine if Michael Jordan had told Phil Jackson "We don't need you coach, I am the team leader, and we have a copy of your book." I also hear people talking about how they are attaining quota, so they don't really feel like they need help. Just like the NFL who has seen offenses evolve to beat various defenses, sales cultures and buying cultures are ever-changing. I remember when the St. Louis Rams and quarterback Kurt Warner dominated football. The team was called the "Greatest Show on Turf." But it was offensive coordinator Mike Martz, behind the scenes who had the ability to spread defenses out and take advantage of weaknesses. There are a ton of professional sales people out there who are going to compete very well against you as you work towards your personal goals in your career. They are not all goofy product pushers who you will walk all over.

You have read this book and you have probably learned some things that have already helped you in your definition of success and have helped you impact the lives of others. While this book is my life's work, it isn't good enough to just read this book and move on. Those who are trying to reach new personal growth heights or who want different results, need to take the next step. To be the best, you need to step up your game. You need a Phil Jackson or Mike Martz to help you navigate through the maze of professional sales.

Lebron James grew up just south of Cleveland, Ohio in Akron and was a Cleveland Cavaliers fan. In 2003, he was drafted by Cavs, right out of high school as the number one pick in the draft. The Cavs had been mediocre, at best, for as long as I could remember. Lebron's impact was immediate as the team began to see success like it had not seen. Lebron was carrying the Cavs further than they had ever gone in previous seasons. Eventually, he took them to the finals multiple times, but they just could not get it done. Lebron was frustrated with the owner of the team, because ownership was not investing in players who could help the team compete with the best programs in the league. It was apparent the ownership's goals were different than his. Yes, the owner would have claimed he wanted a world championship, but his actions proved he wasn't willing to invest to get there. Lebron didn't just want to bring a world championship to Cleveland, he wanted to dominate.

Lebron left Cleveland and signed with the Miami Heat, a team that was willing to invest in players, and Lebron won two World Titles with a very talented team. Still Lebron wanted more. He was willing to go against the norm and put in the work needed to get the results he desired. In 2014, he returned to Cleveland and the owner invested in other great talent to surround him. In 2015, Lebron lead the Cav's to a World Championship beating the Golden State Warriors, who were considered to be the best team that year.

Those who are chasing their dream, who are chasing different results, don't do the status quo. They invest in becoming the best because there is always someone else who will show up and steal your world championship when you grow complacent. This is why I am encouraging you to take the next step and hire a sales coach. Go find the person who can help you take yourself to new heights. But only do it if you are going to go for it. Don't waste your time and money, if you are just going to be a pretender. If you are a pretender, you are done reading the book. Glean from these chapters what you can and I hope it helps you in some way. Those who are serious about their success as defined in Chapter One are the ones ready to surge forward.

First, you need to understand the difference between sales training, mentoring, and coaching. You will find those who claim to be sales coaches, but they are really sales trainers. You will find some who claim to be sales coaches, and all they do is mentor. You will find lots of organizations who do sales training centered around various sales beliefs and methodologies. Let me explain the difference between the three:

- *Training* is when someone teaches you concepts that you may or may not have known before. They teach you the mechanics of the golf swing.
- *Mentoring* is when someone speaks from their experience to give you advise. They share with you what club they would use in a given situation and why. Mentoring can be useful, but it can also be handicapping, if you get stuck always relying on their

opinions to move forward and not learning to think for yourself.

- *Coaching* is when someone helps you think through the situation to find the correct answer for you without leading you to an answer based on their personal experiences, thoughts, and feelings. They ask you questions about the situation to help you decide what you should do in that situation on the golf course without needing someone in your ear before every shot.

We, as a society, have become confused with the definition of a coach because of the sports coaching phenomenon. Athletic coaches are, all too often, trainers and mentors who train you and then show you how to do it. You repeat the process over and over hoping to get the desired results. While all the players on the basketball court know the proper form and play structure, they don't all run it to perfection even though they have been practicing and learning with the same people. All too often, we work for sales managers who are similar to sport coaches. Based on their experience, they tell you what you should do, expecting you to do that very thing. While their intent is to help, they too often handicap you with their advice, preventing you from creating a personal approach to moving forward. I've heard my mentor, Paul Martinelli say, "The greatest gift you can give someone is the gift of thought." Any robot can follow command lines to get a result. Training and mentoring alone often take thought away, while coaching brings you the ability to "self-solve" the situation with clarity and confidence.

All three aspects have a place in your personal development going forward. I am not trying to say you should forgo training and mentoring moving forward only with a coach. On the contrary, I am trying to make sure you don't get stuck with training and mentoring only. True growth won't happen until you learn to think for yourself and to get out of your own way. In my life, that person who helped me to have clarity in my beliefs and thoughts so that my actions were performed naturally at my best, also helped me to grow exponentially. Anyone can hand you ingredients with a recipe and enable you to cook edible food, but it is when you learn how all those ingredients work together, that you can begin to create new dishes.

This is why you need to find a person or maybe several people who can help fill the need for all three of these fronts for you. I personally am a trainer, mentor, and coach. I do not combine the sessions. When I work with someone, I will provide them tools for training (like this book). When mentoring, I will field adhoc calls to show someone how I would handle a specific issue, but for the most part, I am a coach. I help my clients resolve challenges using the brilliant, intelligent mind God created in each of us.

At the end of each chapter, I tried to help you think by giving you some points of reflection. The potential change at this point is squarely in your hands. Have you worked through those reflection points? Have you questioned your process, your language, and put intention to your daily steps and plan? It's not an easy thing to always do on your own. If you have tried and feel you are struggling, a coach can help. Don't hesitate to reach out to me and I can introduce you to some of the best trainers, mentors, and coaches in the industry. I want to make sure you have the opportunity to invest in the future you desire.

Old Thinking: *"I am a professional, I know what to do."*

New Thinking: *"Because I am striving to be my best, I need a coach to help be continue to grow."*

Reflection for the Sales Representative:

1. What leads you to believe you do or don't need a coach? Many times reps say they can't afford it. *I invested 6k my first year to make 150k. Not a bad return on my investment.* Be clear with yourself, because at the end of the day you have to answer to you!
2. What forms of sales training are you doing regularly? If you don't have a plan or if you are not paying for a program, you can change that by putting intentionality to a plan.
3. Find a mentor who can help. Just don't let it become your only source of help.

Reflection for the Sales Manager:

1. Are you a mentor or are you a coach? How can you foster more coaching and less mentorship with your reps?
2. Do you have a coach? Those who are not growing cannot help others grow. Some of my best coaching clients are sales managers who saw their careers grow when they realized they didn't have to know it all or be the smartest person in the room.
3. It's okay to realize your role is not to be the trainer, mentor, and coach. It's okay to pull in help to enable your team to have a safe place to grow without the "boss" factor. How can you create a safe place for personal growth and vulnerability of your reps?

LEAVING YOU WITH THIS

For me it began with toes sticking out of a pair of well-worn shoes. I decided at an early age, I wanted more for myself and my family. My kids were never going to be taunted in school because of tattered clothes or holes in their shoes. With an entrepreneurial spirit rising up inside me, I was drawn to business. I admired those who worked hard and were rewarded for their effort. I had defined success as the financial bottomline on a ledger sheet. Then John Maxwell opened my eyes to a new definition of success. A definition that included helping others to succeed. The focus was no longer just on me and the size of my commission check. I recognized that if I helped others to attain success, I could reap financial rewards. This isn't just a gimmick to increase the size of a paycheck, this is about making those around you taste victory. Thanks for joining me as I shared some of the insights I've discovered working with some of the greatest coaches, mentors, teachers, managers, and sales reps in the industry. Now on to helping many clients on your road to success!

About the Author

Brandon Jeffress is an accomplished sales professional, leader, speaker and coach who has helped hundreds of organizational leaders, entrepreneurs, and sales professionals achieve phenomenal sales results. His clients will tell you that his passion is helping others reach their goals, grow and find significance in their careers. Brandon's desire to invest in others comes from his mentors that include his father, John C. Maxwell and the John Maxwell Team leaders and faculty.

As an entrepreneur and President of JumpSetter, Brandon implements what he preaches. His teachings, writings, and best practices come from many years of being in the trenches learning from his successes and failures. His stories come from real life experiences. His ability to connect with people through these stories is what have drawn so many to seek his guidance.

JumpSetter Philosophy

JumpSetter is a tailored sales engagement approach built around a proven process. We believe that sustainable change happens when thinking changes – and that's what our programs do.

Our customized programming unleashes executive and sales teams' potential and emboldens members to sell more and sell better. We design the structure and processes needed for success.

For more information, contact:

info@jumpsetter.com

Made in the USA
San Bernardino, CA
29 January 2019